CREATING A SUCCESSFUL

Youth
RETREAT

Eight Steps to a Well-Planned Experience

Perhaps the most effective way to create a life-changing Christian experience is with a retreat. My friend Mark Furlan not only leads incredible retreats, he has now given us a most excellent practical guide to make any retreat even more successful. This book is a resource you need in your library.

> Jim Burns, Ph.D.
> President, *YouthBuilders*

Creating a Successful Youth Retreat is wonderful. I will use it to teach others and to recommend to even experienced retreat leaders your sound principles and logical explanations of the framework that makes a great retreat. It is so good I wish I had written it, but I would not have done as good a job. Mark, you have ministered and touched lots of people's lives. Now you will continue to touch even more.

> Ben Innes, O.F.M.
> Guardian of Mission San Luis Rey,
> International Youth Speaker, Retreat Director

CREATING A SUCCESSFUL

Youth
RETREAT

Eight Steps to a Well-Planned Experience

MARK J. FURLAN

ThomasMore®
– An RCL Company –

Allen, Texas

You may contact the author by E-mail at **creativeministries@cox.net**

Acknowledgments:

The Scripture quotations contained herein are from the New Revised Standard Version Bible: Catholic Edition, copyright © 1993 and 1989 by the Division of Christian Education for the National Council of the Churches of Christ in the U.S.A. Used by permission. All rights reserved.

Send all inquiries to:
Thomas More® Publishing
An RCL Company
200 East Bethany Drive
Allen, Texas 75002-3804

Telephone: 800-264-0368 / 972-390-6300
Fax: 800-688-8356 / 972-390-6560

Visit us at: **www.thomasmore.com**
Customer Service E-mail: **cservice@rcl-enterprises.com**

Printed in the United States of America

Library of Congress Control Number: 2002094858

7499   ISBN 0-88347-499-9

1 2 3 4 5   07 06 05 04 03

To my wonderful family,
my wife Kathy and our three children,
Tom, Mark, and Melissa.
If I didn't have your love, support, and encouragement
over twenty years of ministry,
this book would never have been written.
You have made my ministry
a truly rewarding and memorable experience.

ACKNOWLEDGMENTS

In step 8 of this book, I write about the need for dedicated volunteers and the support of the parish community. Without the help of so many great volunteers, I would never have been able to create a successful retreat experience. At the risk of missing a few names, I would like to thank some people who were there for the retreatants year after year: Linda and Ben Benjamin, Mary Jo and Bruce Stelzer, Patti and Darryl Tarullo, Peter Steenblock, Larry and Mary Calkins, Mike Ernst, Mike Rzeznick, Jerry and Martha Tintle, Sharon Burkette, Lori Losey, Tom Bernard, Sr., Ron McDonald, Jim and Jean LaBaugh, Velma Hopkins, and Johnny "G" Giovenelli.

I would also like to acknowledge some of the youth who came back as young adults and were dedicated to working retreats: Eric Julian, Jason Daluiski, Sophia Pac, Maryann Hruz, Chantal Soudant, Tom Calkins, Michelle Roux, Mark Tintle, Brother Al Vu, Heather (Priest) Underwood, Allison Benjamin, Ted Bromley, Donald Calkins, and Michelle Tarullo.

And finally, I would like to thank all the young people who came back time after time to experience a creative retreat.

CONTENTS

INTRODUCTION

After twenty-plus years in ministry, my greatest joy is still planning and directing retreats. Naturally, as a youth minister, most of the retreats I was involved with were for high-school-age youth groups. I have also directed retreats for staff development, eighth grade graduation retreats, young adults, parents of teenagers, leadership development, junior high youth ministry, RCIA teams, Confirmation and discernment weekends for volunteers, just to mention a few. I mention this variety of retreats I have planned and directed only to emphasize the broad scope of possibilities in doing retreats once you understand the process of planning for a great retreat experience.

This book will take you through the eight steps to creating a great retreat. In the big picture, the process I use may have elements that you are already using. The greatest difference for me, however, has been in paying attention to the details associated to each of these steps. Let me give you an example.

We all need a team if we are going to direct a retreat of any size or for a retreat that lasts more than a few hours. But what are the qualities you look for in selecting a team member? What expectations do you have for these people? What role do you want each of them to play in the retreat? The more detail you put into recruiting volunteers for the retreat, the greater your chances of having a successful experience for the retreatants. In other words, do you *settle* on whoever volunteers, or do you *select* your team?

This book is laid out in what I feel is the order of priorities. The first four steps deal with the components found in a good retreat. Naturally, not every retreat will have all of these components. My goal here is to give you a broad view of what is possible, so that before you make a selection of what elements you will include in the retreat, each of your choices has a purpose.

Step 5 deals with how to put these components together in a well thought out manner. Playing games, the celebration of Mass, Reconciliation, a skit or music—each should have a purpose. They should not be used as fillers between meals and talks. Step 5 also helps us manage time properly. I am a strong believer that once we have been given the gift of the retreatants' time we should use this time to the full advantage for a successful retreat experience.

Steps 6 and 7 address the challenge of training retreat team members to be prepared and have a sense of confidence in fulfilling their role on the retreat. Small-group facilitating, listening skills, communication skills, and preparing talks are covered in these Steps. The more input the team has in planning for the retreat, and the better trained they are, the more ownership they take in the success of the overall retreat.

In Step 8 we will look at living in a parish community. My experiences as a youth minister has proved to me time and time again that the parish wants the youth to have a strong youth ministry program that includes a quality retreat component. If the pastor, the parents, and the community at large see results, they are more than willing to support you and your program in many other ways. The first challenge in renewing the parish vision of youth ministry depends on our role as advocates. In this step I will share my experiences in making this happen.

The final section of the book covers a few miscellaneous topics and contains copies of retreat applications, parent letters, medical release forms, and other assorted documents and details that I hope will assist you in stimulating your own ideas.

After directing over one hundred fifty retreats to thousands of youth over the years, I have found that whenever I get the chance to get together with these kids now as adults, the conversation takes us down memory lane. It never fails that eventually the topic they will turn to is that of their retreat experiences. It is as a result of these conversations with so many of "my" kids that I decided to write this book—because so many of them encouraged me to do so.

By consistently using these eight steps to creating a great retreat experience, and through the guidance of the Holy Spirit, I can honestly say that I have never been associated with a poor retreat. I firmly believe that this process that has worked for me for so many years can work for others as well.

Step One
CREATING THE PLAN

☐ Introduction

☐ Selecting a Retreat Location

☐ Transportation

☐ Selecting a Team

☐ Retreat Team Qualities

☐ Retreat Team Expectations

☐ Retreat Team Positions

☐ Retreat Team Meeting Schedule

GETTING STARTED

I begin each retreat by telling the retreatants my philosophy of what I think a retreat should be. The analogy I use is that of a road trip my family of five and I took from Southern California to Vancouver, British Columbia, Canada. The trip north alone took us three days, so as you can guess we spent a lot of time in the van. Periodically, we would pull off the road at state-provided comfort stations or rest stops. At these rest stops we would get out of the van to stretch our legs, get some fresh water, and maybe even have a little picnic. The driver could rest and the children would run and play. Before we got back on the road, we would clean all the trash out of the van, and take a look at the map to be sure that we were heading in the right direction.

To me, a retreat is like a comfort station or rest stop on the road of life. A retreat gives us a chance to stop and stretch our spirit, nourish our souls, and rest and play. It should give us an opportunity to get rid of some of the clutter and mess in our lives. And lastly, it should provide us with the tools to make needed adjustments on our map for the next part of our life journey.

Before we get to the point of providing a retreat experience that allows this to happen, a great deal of preparation work must take place. This step covers most of the groundwork that you as a retreat director will need to do before your first team meeting. This includes reserving a location, booking transportation, selecting a team, and preparing a retreat team schedule.

Throughout this book I will try to cover as many details as I can to give you helpful information in each area of planning. Because everyone's situation and program is a little different, you may find parts of some steps to be unnecessary information for you. That's okay with me. If all your retreats are at the church, for example, the information in the step on selecting a location and transportation will not apply, but the information on selecting a team is important if you want a smooth-flowing retreat experience.

SELECTING A RETREAT LOCATION

E arly in my ministry I changed parishes. Prior to beginning work at the new parish, I had a series of meetings with the youth minister who was leaving. During our conversation we talked about the retreat program. He told me he had reservations at a location for the second weekend in November. To his credit, I have to say he was partially right. When I called the retreat center I found that he had made reservations. Unfortunately, no deposit had been sent to hold the reservation. Consequently, the reservation had been canceled and the facility rented to another group. It was early August and I found myself frantically trying to find a location for a fall retreat.

After a week of contacting every retreat center, camp, and church organization within a ninety-mile radius of our parish, I finally found a conference center run by the Boy Scouts of America. I felt like I had hit the jackpot when I heard the description of the facilities. The friendly staff members told me about the conference room with two fireplaces, a lake for swimming, a large grass field for outside games, a rope course, and even a chapel. They also offered a choice of chicken or steak for our Saturday night dinner. The price was a little more than I wanted to pay, but taking into consideration the great facility, the availability on the already-published date of the second weekend in November, and that this was the only positive response after days of phone calls, I said yes. I reserved the center, ordered thirty-five chicken dinners and thirty-five steak dinners for Saturday night, and set out to plan the rest of the details of the weekend. The youth who signed up for the retreat were very excited about the center and their adventures ahead. That was the good news.

On Friday, the first day of the retreat, I arrived at the conference center about six hours before the retreatants were expected to arrive, so that I could get everything set up. I met with the center director who showed me around the grounds. The dorms were nice, with plenty of hot water. The kitchen and dining area were large, and they provided us with coffee, tea, water, and juice all weekend. They would even have freshly baked cookies ready for the kids when they got off the bus.

Next he showed me the chapel . . . the *personal* chapel. This newly painted chapel was only big enough for less than ten people, not the seventy that would be arriving soon. As we entered the eighty-year-old adobe conference center, the director pointed out the damage the fireplace had sustained in the most recent earthquake. We wouldn't be able to use it. He said we could have a fire in the other fireplace, but it would have to be small because the chimney was so full of soot that smoke often backed up into the room and set off the fire alarms.

From the conference center he took me outside to the large grass field . . . with the broken fence. The hole in the fence allowed the cows from the neighboring pasture to come in and graze. As with most animals, what goes in one end must come out the other. I will leave it to your own imagination to figure out what the field was like.

The lake was covered in moss and other stuff that grows in and around stagnant water so the swimsuits packed in the retreatants' suitcases would have to go unused. The rope course, the director told me, would be five dollars extra per person if we brought our own guide and ten dollars each if we used one of theirs. Finally, as I learned later, the thirty-five steak dinners I ordered would add an additional four dollars per person, costing me an additional $140.00 over my budget.

I would love to be able to tell you that I made up this story just to make a point, but unfortunately it is true. I must also add that after they made a few repairs to the facilities and I learned to stick with the menu that was offered, I returned to this center with future retreats a number of times and thoroughly enjoyed it.

So what did I learn from this and other experiences in selecting a location for a retreat? It's probably obvious by now that I should personally have visited the center far in advance of the actual retreat date. But that is only one step. Listed below are a few questions that you should ask before selecting a location for your retreat:

❐ Are there any extra charges for special additions to the regularly offered prices? Is use of the pool extra? Is firewood for fire pit or fireplace extra? If they have priests available for sacraments, is there an additional charge?

❐ Do they provide snacks and drinks all weekend?

❐ Will you be sharing the facilities with other groups? If the answer is yes, find out who they are and if the other group will be comfortable with your youth group present. Also, check to see if you will be eating together with other groups. If the answer is yes, how will this affect grace, cleanup, and any party decorations you may have planned to celebrate a special meal.

❐ Does the center have a noise curfew?

❐ Do they have a chapel? How big is it? Do you have to reserve it for (1) Masses or prayer services, (2) small-group prayer, and (3) private devotion and meditation?

❐ Are they comfortable with your using the chapel for talks and presentations and small-group sharing?

❐ If you are planning to include a Mass, do you have to bring everything, or do they have vestments, Sacramentary, Lectionary, and chalice, etc.?

- ❐ Are meal times flexible to fit your schedule, or are they set by the cook?

- ❐ Do they have private accommodations for your director or a priest?

- ❐ Are snacks and drinks allowed in the conference room and/or dorms?

- ❐ Is it okay to tape posters, signs, etc. on the walls?

- ❐ Do they provide a stereo or sound system, or do you have to bring your own? Does it take CD's or tapes?

- ❐ What is the environment in the conference room? If you expect the retreatants to sit on the floor, ask if the room is carpeted. If you need them, are there tables and chairs? Is there an extra charge for them?

- ❐ Do they provide linens or are you expected to bring your own?

- ❐ What is the menu for the weekend? Do you have choices? Spaghetti will be a far better choice than tuna casserole for example!

- ❐ Will the cook accommodate special diets? Are vegetarian meals provided?

- ❐ Always take the time to tour the facilities well in advance of the retreat.

Finally, it is always better to make your reservations early rather than late. In Southern California, for example, retreat centers are in great demand and should be reserved at least a year in advance. Remember to always check with your students' high schools before you select a date and book a retreat center. It is important to avoid conflicts like homecoming, finals, SAT's, proms, winter formals, spring break, etc.

TRANSPORTATION

M any think that the retreat begins when the retreatants have loaded their gear into their dorms and are assembled in the conference room for the first exercise of the retreat. This is an unfortunate misconception. I have always considered the retreat to begin when the retreatants board the bus or van with the other members of the retreat and begin their journey together to the retreat center. Transportation to and from a retreat or any other youth ministry event can be a problem if you haven't planned properly for it.

The options for transportation are limited to two; order a bus, or organize a group of parents to drive. Whichever option you choose, you first should check with your diocese regarding rules and liabilities. If you are going to rent a bus or coach, they may have an approved list of vendors from which you can choose. If you are using adults as drivers, the diocese may have guidelines or rules regarding age, insurance requirements, criminal background checks, or limits per vehicle. I have not found a diocese that would approve of a youth group member driving to a retreat.

I would also encourage you to talk to your pastor to see how he feels about transportation. His preference might be for you to use a bus rather than private vehicles. If that's the case, he may even be willing for the parish to pay for the cost of the bus as a gift from the community. He might also recommend other resources that might be willing to pay for all or part of the bus. This is covered more thoroughly in Step 8.

Taking a Bus?

If you choose to take a bus, I recommend that you start collecting price quotes at least six months before the retreat. Three quotes should give you an idea of the price and help you with the budgeting for the retreat.

In chartering a bus it is always good to ask a few questions. Here are some things you will need to know:

- ❐ Size of the Bus: Don't pay for a fifty-five-passenger bus when all you have is thirty-five passengers. The reverse is also true. If you need a fifty-five-passenger bus, make sure that is what you are ordering. Don't charter a bus just because the price is best. Always check the size.

- ❐ When you talk about size, also ask about storage. If you are planning for fifty-five people, the bus should be able to hold fifty-five sleeping bags and fifty-five-plus pieces of luggage. If you don't think the bus has enough storage space, see if you can find a parent with a full-size pickup truck or van who would be willing to help with this task.

- ❐ Does the company allow food or drink on the bus?

- ❐ Does the driver help with loading and unloading the luggage? In my experience they will usually help supervise, but you should assign a few people to load and unload the bus.

- ❐ If you are planning to stop on the way to and/or from the retreat, let's say for a meal or a bathroom break, does the company charge for the extra stops?

- ❐ What will the bus company do for you in case a bus breaks down on the way to or from the retreat?

- ❐ Will the company bill you, or will you need to pay the driver with a check?

Taking Private Vehicles?

If you choose to use private vehicles using parent or other adult drivers, start planning for this two or three months before the retreat. Do yourself a favor and find a reliable parent or team of parents to coordinate this task for you. You don't need to be dealing with canceled drivers thirty-six or forty-eight hours before the retreat. Let a parent who wants to contribute to the experience but can't get away for the weekend do this for you. Here is a list of questions to ask when looking for drivers:

- ❒ Are you at least twenty-five years old? This seems to be the minimum acceptable age in most dioceses.

- ❒ Do you have insurance?

- ❒ Don't ask how many people they can carry, ask how many seat-belts are in their vehicle. That's how many people they can carry.

- ❒ If you are going to the mountains, is the driver comfortable and familiar with driving on mountain roads (maybe in the dark, snow, or bad weather)?

- ❒ Is your vehicle adequate for mountain roads with steep upward and downward slopes?

- ❒ Can you drive both ways? Maybe some people can only drive to the retreat and others are only available to pick up at the end of the retreat. Make sure this is clarified ahead of time.

- ❒ A parent with a truck or cargo van can be helpful to carry sleeping bags, luggage, etc.

- ❒ Have all drivers meet at the church, even if they are picking up all their passengers at another location, like at school.

It is always helpful to let drivers know up front what is expected of them regarding timing and responsibility. You should provide all drivers with a detailed map, medical release forms for each passenger, and phone numbers for a contact at the parish and at the retreat center in case of emergency.

To avoid any last-minute surprises, call your bus company and/or adult drivers about forty-eight hours before you plan to leave for the retreat to confirm all the arrangements.

RETREAT TEAM POSITIONS

(Some positions will overlap)

Director: _____

    ❑ The primary responsibility is to plan the retreat and the preparation of the retreat team.

    ❑ The director facilitates the retreat during the retreat, ensuring the smooth flow of the experience.

    ❑ Together with the team, the director discerns the "spirit" of the group, individual retreatants, and the direction the retreat is going.

Assistant Director: _____

    ❑ The assistant director works with the director in planning retreat team meeting agendas.

    ❑ He/she also assists the director with any logistics required for the smooth flow of the retreat and fills in for the director on the weekend if the director is called away by an emergency or by a retreatant or team member.

    ❑ The assistant director sometimes acts as "go-fer" before or during the retreat.

Program Director: _____

    ❑ The program director assures the smooth flow of the retreat by having all needed materials available at the designated times and places. (I have only used a program director on a few occasions, usually when the size of the group or layout of the retreat location dictated the need for an extra set of hands.)

Spiritual Director: _____

❑ Optional and should be limited to a trained spiritual director or pastoral counselor. The person filling this position should not be assigned to a group in order to be available to the retreatants for spiritual direction or pastoral counseling throughout the retreat. I encourage the spiritual director to be present for and join in all activities of the weekend. This helps the spiritual director to be sensitive to the tone of the talks, the sharing, the retreat in general, and, most especially, the individual retreatants.

Speaker(s): _____

❑ Number of speakers will vary according to the retreat plan.

❑ Provide the "meat" of the retreat in that he/she then gives prepared presentations on a specific topic. Each presentation includes input, a reflection, a sharing, and a celebration.

Liturgist: _____

❑ Coordinates all prayer services (morning prayers, night prayers, grace before and after meals, paraliturgies, etc.)

❑ This person is not a priest or deacon, but a layperson, even youth, who is familiar with the processes of prayer and liturgical services.

Musician: _____

❑ Provides music and leads singing for liturgies, prayer services, etc.

Audio/Visual Technician: _____

❑ Sets up sound system, coordinates music at designated times, and sets up any other technical equipment for Power Point.

❑ Presentations, video recording of retreat, etc.

Facilitators: _____

❑ Facilitate small-group activities and take part in all retreat activities.

RETREAT TEAM QUALITIES

For many retreat team members, they are chosen to be on the team by virtue of the fact that they are living, breathing people who tentatively raised their hand at a meeting or checked a box on a volunteer form. These are probably not be best criteria by which to choose the people who will have so great an impact on your retreat, and more importantly, on your retreatants. Here are some suggestions that may help in choosing effective retreat team members:

- ❐ Make sure this person has a commitment to the youth, to the purpose of the retreat, and is able to attend all retreat team meetings and be present for the entire retreat.

- ❐ Whether you are planning a retreat for junior high, senior high, young adults, or a group of single parents, retreat team members need to be able to interact effectively with the maturity level of the retreatants.

- ❐ Because a retreat forces a person to look inwardly, a team member must be able to respond to the retreatants with compassion, sensitivity, caring, and Gospel values.

- ❐ A team member needs to be able to work with others as a team and be able to take directions.

- ❐ This person must have the dedication and dependability to do what they say they will do, when they say they will do it. This is important during the planning as they follow through on their assigned tasks, but doubly important on the retreat itself, to maintain the flow of the retreat.

☐ It is vital that all team members have a good sense of their own spiritual journey with God.

☐ It is very important that, regardless of personal viewpoints, team members do not deviate from the teachings of the Magisterium of the church when interacting with the youth.

☐ Team members must have good communication skills, not only in speaking, but more importantly in listening.

RETREAT TEAM EXPECTATIONS

Your retreat team begins as a blank slate, and each team will develop a unique personality of its own. There are some basic expectations that should be common to all retreat teams, expectations that will form a firm foundation for your team:

☐ A retreat team is a community of believers who have come together to create a retreat experience for others. It is important to be an example of Christ's love, compassion, and understanding as we work together in planning the experience and live together on the retreat.

☐ We are called to serve. The retreatants are the most important part of the retreat. If we believe these first two statements, then we, as the team, must remember that we are there to serve the retreatants. A person should not be selected as a team member because *they* need the experience or because they have a friend on the team or a relative going to the retreat.

☐ The Holy Spirit chooses when to speak, and through whom he chooses to speak. Each team member is expected to listen to other team members. Sometimes this may be difficult, especially when conflicting ideas start to flow at a team meeting. If we expect to be heard, then we must give each member our total attention.

☐ Finally, I would like to caution you in selecting people to be team members who have their own agendas. An example may be someone who offers to work on a youth ministry retreat because they believe that youth today have no respect for Mary and want to teach them to pray the rosary correctly. Unless this is a theme of the retreat, I wouldn't include this person as a team member, as they can potentially disrupt the flow of the retreat, constantly interjecting their own agenda.

RETREAT TEAM MEETING SCHEDULE

R etreat team meetings are a time for the team to develop from individuals into a team, for planning, brainstorming, and dedicating the retreat to the Lord. We begin and end each team meeting in prayer, and then move on to the tasks for that evening.

Week 1   ❒ Introduction

            ❒ Philosophy of Retreats

            ❒ Retreat Team Positions

            ❒ Team Expectations

            ❒ Retreat Theme

            ❒ Retreat Song

Week 2   ❒ Retreat Theme

            ❒ Retreat Song

            ❒ Review Retreat Applications

            ❒ Input Topics

            ❒ "How to Write a Talk"

Week 3   ❒ "How to Write a Talk"

            ❒ Retreat Schedule

            ❒ Spiritual Exercises

Week 4   ❑   Retreat Schedule

             ❑   Retreat Job Descriptions

Week 5   ❑   Communication Skills

             ❑   Small Group Facilitating

Week 6   ❑   Listening Skills

             ❑   Progress Reports on Assigned Tasks

             ❑   Talk Presentations

Week 7   ❑   Talk Presentations

             ❑   Progress Reports on Assigned Tasks

Week 8   ❑   Final Preparation

             ❑   Last-Minute Stuff

By the end of the eight weeks of preparation, the team members are firmly dedicated to the retreatants and to the success of the weekend. Team members who have never worked on a retreat before feel empowered, confident, and eager to journey with the retreatants through the exciting experience that lies ahead.

CREATING THE IDENTITY OF THE RETREAT

☐ Retreat Themes

☐ Topics for Presentations

☐ Selecting Music

RETREAT THEMES

I believe in naming retreats, giving each retreat a character and identity of its own. The name is drawn from the theme, which sets the foundation for the direction of the retreat. Most of my retreat themes include the words "discover" or "experience" in the title: "Discover the Peace," "Discover the Journey," "Experience God's Love," etc. Using "discover" or "experience" in the theme implies action; something is going to happen on the retreat.

During one retreat preparation the team was having trouble picking a theme and deciding whether to use the word "discover" or "experience." Someone suggested, "How about 'Discover the Experience'?" The suggestion was made tongue-in-cheek, but after a short discussion, we went with it.

Be careful, however, not to let the theme *overpower* the direction of the retreat. For example, let's say the theme is "Discover the Spirit." You wouldn't necessarily have all your talks center on the Spirit: "The Gifts of the Spirit," "The Fruits of the Spirit," The Spirit As Part of the Trinity," "The Spirit of our Community," "We Are One in the Spirit," "The Spirit Flows Through Me," "The Spirit in My Life." You get the idea. As in all elements of the retreat, the theme, talk topics, prayer services, etc., must have balance.

The choices available for selecting a theme are only limited by the imagination of your team. Over the years I have used song titles, book titles, movie titles, quotes, current events, and, of course, scripture passages.

My first step in looking for ideas for a retreat theme is to read and meditate on the daily readings scheduled for all the days of the retreat. Next, I take a look at both the liturgical and seasonal calendars for ideas. Here is a list of retreat topics, broken down by seasons and liturgical events for the traditional school year. I have found these to be helpful in choosing retreat themes:

Fall: September, October, November

Early fall is a great time to have a retreat. It sets the spiritual tone for the group and lays a good foundation for building community for the rest of the year. It also allows for adequate opportunity to follow up on the theme through the year. Caution: before you schedule the weekend, be sure it doesn't conflict with your local high schools' homecoming weekends or other major fall activities.

The season of fall lends itself to many traditional retreat theme topics such as harvest, thanksgiving, life, and Homecoming: Feeling at Home with Jesus. Themes can be found in the scripture readings for the week, or even in holidays and feast days found in the calendar.

September

Beginning a New School Year. New Beginnings, Change.
21 St. Matthew the Apostle
27 St. Vincent De Paul

October

4   St. Francis of Assisi
7   Our Lady of the Rosary
12 Columbus Day—Discover!
18 St. Luke the Evangelist
28 St. Simon and Jude
31 Halloween

November

1   All Saints Day
2   All Souls Day

21   Presentation of the Virgin Mary
22   St. Cecilia—Music
      Feast of Christ the King
      Thanksgiving
30   St. Andrew the Apostle, Brother of Peter
      Advent: Hope, Waiting

Winter: December, January, February

A winter retreat provides a great opportunity to escape from the cold and darkness of the season and provides a happy change of pace. Once again, before you lock in your retreat dates, check with the school for conflicting activities—finals, winter formal, etc.

December
      Advent
  6   St. Nicholas—Giving
  8   Immaculate Conception of Mary
 12   Our Lady of Guadalupe

Planning anything from December 15 through the first week of January could be tough. If you do plan a retreat during Christmas break, the primary themes are of course, Christmas, St. Stephen's Day, the Feast of St. John the Evangelist, and the Feast of the Holy Family. Be sure you have a solid commitment from your retreatants (paperwork and payment) if you plan a retreat during this time, or the lure of other holiday activities may mean many empty spaces at your retreat.

January
  1   Mary the Mother of God
  4   St. Elizabeth Ann Seton—First American Saint
      Epiphany of the Lord
      Baptism of Jesus

Martin Luther King's Birthday
25 Conversion of St. Paul
Catholic Schools Week

February
12 Valentines Day
Ash Wednesday
Beginning of Lent
Presidents' Day—Leadership

Spring: March, April, May

A spring retreat presents us with all that spring has to offer: planting of seeds, new life, new beginning, and resurrection. It can be used to anticipate the approaching end of the school year, graduation and Confirmation. During this season be aware of SAT's the prom, spring break, and other major school events.

March
Lent
Palm Sunday
Stations of the Cross
Tridium (Holy Thursday, Good Friday, Holy Saturday)
Easter
19 St. Joseph's Day
25 Annunciation of the Lord

April
Lent
Palm Sunday
Stations of the Cross
Tridium (Holy Thursday, Good Friday, Holy Saturday)
Easter
25 St. Mark the Evangelist
29 St. Catherine of Sienna

May

> Easter Season
> Ascension of the Lord (40 days after Easter)
> 14   St. Matthias
> Pentecost Sunday
> Holy Trinity Sunday
> 31   Visitation of the Virgin Mary to Elizabeth

As the team goes through the brainstorming process of selecting a theme it is important for the director to allow every idea to be heard. The more lively the discussion, the more ideas begin to flow and the greater the final list of suggestions to choose from. At times I have ended up with a list of fifteen to twenty-five theme suggestions from the team. The final decision in selecting the theme belongs to the team. This enables them to take ownership of the retreat experience. (I must admit that in all these years of directing retreats, only twice has the team selected my suggestion for the theme.)

I never get rid of the rejected theme ideas, but roll them over as a starting block for the process of selecting topics for the talks. An idea may not have been strong enough for the theme, but may be a catalyst for a great talk.

TOPICS FOR PRESENTATION

After years of asking youth what topics they want to learn about on retreat, I have found that the requests fall into four basic categories:

❑ Spiritual—Your relationship with God.

❑ Personal—About ourselves.

❑ Relational—How do we deal with others in a one-on-one relationship?

❑ Communal—How do we deal with living in a community; family, school, parish?

A good retreat experience for youth should always cover spiritual, personal, relational, and communal aspects. If the retreat theme lends itself, I encourage you to include one talk from each of the four areas. I always include a talk about community in an early fall retreat. This helps build a sense of community in the youth ministry program that carries on throughout the school year. On retreats, the talks are like the meat of a meal, and the small-group sharing is like the potatoes. Remember, these presentations are not designed to impress the retreatants with someone's great speaking skills, but as springboards for growth and introspection. They are followed by silent reflection, and then by small-group sharing.

Catechetical, topical, or informational are three other categories for talk topics. Catechetical talks address the teachings of the church or the Magisterium of the church. Topics that fall under this category are often used for sacramental preparation, such as

Confirmation retreats. I caution you, however, against planning a strictly catechetical retreat experience for students of any age. If you use a catechetical topic, use it early in the retreat, and then let the spiritual, personal, relational, and communal build on it in a personal and reflective way.

Topical or informational talks deal with the issues of the day. Two weeks before one of my retreats was scheduled to begin, two boys from a local high school were killed in a car accident. The team felt we should discuss the topic of death during the retreat to help give the retreatants an opportunity to put closure on the deaths of their classmates and friends in a safe, spiritual environment. We did this by changing the schedule and adding the talk followed by small-group sharing. We closed the reflection with a spiritual exercise that included a prayer service for the two boys, as well as for other deaths in the retreatants' families. It was a time of tears, and a time of healing, brought about by including a topic of the day in the retreat experience.

Once I had a young man in my program attempt suicide two days before a retreat. I knew this topic was going to be fresh in the minds of the retreatants and team. After consulting with a few team members, I made the decision to begin the retreat with a talk on suicide. This gave the retreatants an opportunity to deal with the primary issue on their minds, freeing them to continue the weekend with the agenda of the retreat.

I have listed below a few topics I have used over the years in each of the four primary topical areas. I hope they are helpful to you.

Spiritual Topics

Spiritual topics deal with our relationship with God the Father, God the Son, and God the Holy Spirit. Talks in this category can cover prayer (how we pray, when we pray, forms of prayer, etc.), the sacraments, faith, trust, scripture, the creed, meditation, fasting, listening to God, and many more.

Some other spiritual topics are:

- ❒ When I pray
- ❒ Is That You Speaking, Lord?
- ❒ On My Journey . . .
- ❒ Where Are You God?
- ❒ Finding God in Nature
- ❒ Following Jesus As Healer/Forgiver
- ❒ God's Kingdom on Earth
- ❒ Who Moved? Me or God?
- ❒ Growing Close to God
- ❒ Praying with My Heart Open and My Mouth Shut
- ❒ Knowing God's Will
- ❒ Who Is God?
- ❒ Who Is Jesus?
- ❒ Who Is the Holy Spirit?
- ❒ Prayer: Why It's Important, Why It's Hard, How We Pray.
- ❒ Finding God in My Life
- ❒ Is a Living, Breathing Relationship with God Possible?
- ❒ Sacraments: What Part Do They Play in Our Lives?
- ❒ My Most Significant Steps on the Journey of Faith
- ❒ Following the Teachings of Jesus

❐ Scripture in My Daily Life

❐ The Way, the Truth, and the Life

❐ Your Heart Is Where Your Treasure Is

Relational Topics

It would be practically impossible today to get fifty teenagers in a room on retreat and not have the majority of them struggling in a relationship. If it's not with one of their parents, it's with a sibling. If it isn't a boyfriend/girlfriend relationship problem, it's about their best friend. Whoever the relationship is with, they might not be struggling with it now, but they have in the past, or will in the future. That is why I always try to include a topic having to do with relationships.

Listed below are just a few of the topics I have used in the past. I am sure that you have a list of your own as well. If you don't, just ask your youth group and they will be happy to give you something to work with.

Here are some suggestions:

❐ What Does It Mean to Be a Friend?

❐ The Decision to Date

❐ Getting Along with Parents

❐ Life on Campus

❐ Sex: A Christian Perspective

❐ Now That We're Dating

❐ Making Relationships Work

❐ Communicating with Friends

❐ Respect for Others

❑ Who Am I to Judge?

❑ I Didn't Say That! How We Listen.

❑ Bearing One Another's Burdens

❑ Compassion and Responsibility in a Relationship

❑ Peer Pressure: How to Respond

Personal Topics

The list of topics that fall under personal issues is only limited by the size of your group. As a spiritual director and pastoral counselor with youth, I was always impressed by what they thought about, what was concerning them the most. Given the opportunity in a safe environment, kids are willing to share their fears and dreams, their pain and their joy. The list I am providing for you under personal topics is a little longer than relational or communal, only because I found it hard to choose which ones to leave out:

❑ The Man in the Mirror: How I See Myself

❑ Self-Esteem

❑ Responding to God's Call

❑ Living a Simple Life in a Confusing World

❑ Making Moral Decisions

❑ When My Life Was Challenged, Changed, Strengthened

❑ Don't Worry, Be Faithful

❑ Being a Peacemaker in Today's World

❑ When I Forgave I Was Healed

❑ Recognizing My Special Talents and Gifts

❐ My Life As a Disciple

❐ Happy Are Those Who Are Humble

❐ Happy Are the Pure in Heart

❐ Just Not Good Enough

❐ When I Was Lonely

❐ Our Job Is to Be Christ's Witness

❐ Living What We Believe and Preach (Walking the Talk)

❐ The Art of Humility and Hospitality

❐ Christ Empowers Us to Continue His Work

❐ School Struggles

❐ Understanding Feelings

❐ Uniqueness of the Individual

Communal Topics

If you are finding it difficult to get good communal topics, may I suggest any of Paul's letters? I can't tell you how many times I have gone to his writings to get exactly what I was looking for. Make sure that the person selected for this talk has a broad background of communal experiences to choose from for their personal sharing and witness part of the talk. Communal talks can deal with the community at school, the parish community, or the youth group community, and so on. Some communal topics might include:

❐ Is This Truly a Christian Community?

❐ Using the Gifts of the Holy Spirit As Tools
    to Build Christian Community

❐ Using the Community As a Base for Ministry

❒ The Community Has the Power of Christ's Spirit

❒ The Demands of Community Life

❒ Concerns in the Christian Community

❒ Can I Love God If I Don't Love My Neighbor?

❒ Community: Let's Make It Work

❒ Am I the Future of the Church?

❒ Christ's Presence in the Church Today?

Presentation of topics is not limited to just giving talks. Other ways of presenting a topic can include a dramatic presentation, creating a skit that gets the message across, or a short clip from a movie that covers the topic. On a recent retreat one of the talks dealt with prayer styles. The team came up with showing live examples of prayer instead of just talking about prayer. During their skit, four team members came before the group and, after a very short introduction to set the tone, each demonstrated a different prayer style. Experiencing the variety of prayer styles instead of just hearing about them in a talk freed the retreatants to realize that they can pray in their own styles.

Be creative, use the team's imagination, and don't be afraid to try new things. My youth group complained whenever I got into a pattern, but they were never bored when I stepped out in faith and explored new avenues in presenting the material.

SELECTING MUSIC

M usic plays a large but subtle part of my retreats. My team and I always try to pick a song that speaks to the topic of the theme, and play it a few times on the weekend as a subtle reminder of the theme. I encourage the presenters of talks to select a song to use at the introduction or more importantly at the end of a talk that fits with the objective of the talk. I play instrumental tapes and CD's as a soft backdrop during small-group sharing time. This helps keep the groups focused on the conversation in their own group, and also miraculously sets a ceiling on the level of noise in the room.

I encourage the team to use music during Mass, at prayer services, in skits, and during spiritual exercises. I don't limit the use of music to church hymns or Christian music. I encourage the use of appropriate contemporary music. One warning though about using contemporary music: It is important with some artists' music for you to review the words of the song to assure that they are appropriate. You may even need to watch the music video. Even though the song may be used in the context of the retreat, inappropriate images will come to the consciousness of those who have viewed the video if the music isn't carefully screened.

Choosing contemporary music wisely however can have a positive effect. Youth and adults both have told me that when they have heard a "retreat song" on the radio even long after the retreat, they still reflect back to the talk, prayer service, or to whatever element of the retreat that song touched a chord in their hearts. What more could we ask of today's music, than that it bring someone's mind back to a great retreat experience that brought them closer to God?

Step Three
CREATING VEHICLES FOR THE SPIRIT

☐ Planning Prayer Services

☐ Planning Spiritual Exercises

☐ Planning Liturgies

☐ Sample Liturgy

PLANNING PRAYER SERVICES

Planning for a prayer service doesn't have to be a major undertaking, but, on the other hand, it should not be overlooked either. Good prayer experiences greatly enhance the quality of the overall retreat experience for the participant. Experiencing a variety of prayer styles can help a retreatant find his or her vehicle to connect with God. All prayer services should be planned in advance to reflect the purpose for the prayer or the theme of the weekend. Prayer can also be required to center thoughts and hearts back on the Lord, when transitioning from meals, games, or breaks back to listening to a talk. It can put closure on one segment or open a new segment.

I have always made it a practice on retreats for the entire retreat team to come forward to quietly pray over a speaker just before he or she gives their presentation. We invoke the Holy Spirit to speak God's word to the retreatants and to open their ears and hearts to accept what the Lord has for them in the talk. After the first few talks, the retreatants come to respect this moment, and spontaneously become silent as they begin to realize the significance of the moment. Although this only takes a moment or two, it is included in the schedule so as not to overlook this important element of the retreat.

I assume you have a basic knowledge of planning prayer services. If you do not, there is a wealth of books on the subject available at your Christian bookstore, and I have listed a few resources for you in the appendix at the end of this book. Besides specific resources, there are four key elements to consider when planning retreat prayer services. I hope these will serve as a springboard for your own creativity and spirituality, and that of your team:

❐ *The Written Word*

A reading from scripture, the life of a saint, a poem, something written by one of the retreatants, a section from a book, the lines from a song—all can set the stage for prayer and cause us to reflect.

❐ *Music*

Instrumental music, a contemporary song, a modern Christian song, a traditional hymn, and creative noise—all lend themselves to prayer. One effective use of creative noise happened on one retreat during morning prayer to the Holy Spirit. As the leader of the prayer set the tone of the prayer with a poem about the Holy Spirit, she had a friend outside gently fanning wind chimes. The gentle, light chiming filled the room with just enough sound to create an environment that helped the retreatants feel the presence of the Holy Spirit. Another very effective use of sounds during a prayer service about the never ceasing call of God was a tape playing in the background with the constant sound of waves breaking on the sand.

❐ *Location, Location, Location!*

No, you're not buying a business, you're planning a prayer service. Even if it will only take a few minutes, where will the service be held? Will it be indoors or outdoors? Will you be in small groups or in a large group? Will you be sitting, standing in a circle, holding hands, separated apart from one another? Will you be in the chapel, the conference room, the dining room, or outside under a tree? Picture the location, picture the posture, and what will best lead to a prayerful experience that fits with the purpose of the prayer.

❐ *Environment and Props*

I love using many different things on retreats to set the environment for prayer. I believe the more options to stimulate the senses during prayer, the greater chance I have of meeting the spiritual needs of the group. I have used water, incense, rocks, leaves, grass, candles, fabric, pictures, food, symbols, scented oil—anything I can find that is appropriate to the purpose of the prayer. As much as I encourage you to be creative, I also want to caution you to do is tastefully. You're creating a prayer service, not a birthday party! Another element that effects prayer is lighting. Whether it be bright sunlight, cool shade, firelight, or even indirect lighting with a lamp in the conference room, consider how you can set the mood for the prayer service with lighting.

As I have said before, and will continue to say throughout this book, everything we do has to have a purpose. Too often we include prayers and praying in our schedule just because it is what we as Christians are supposed to do. In Step 1, I provide a list of team positions. In that list you will find a position for a spiritual director and a liturgist. The role of the liturgist is to *coordinate* liturgies, spiritual exercises, and prayer services. I emphasize that they *coordinate* them. The liturgist does not have to do all of them, but must see that whoever is assigned to that task for each service or prayer is prepared before the weekend. This person also needs to make sure that the plan flows with the rest of the progress of the retreat plan, in other words, with what comes before and after that prayer or liturgy.

If you don't have a liturgist, then the responsibilities roll over to the spiritual director or the assistant director. If you don't have a liturgist, spiritual director, or assistant director, then the responsibility falls on the director.

Let's take a closer look at what I mean by having a purpose. The purpose of morning prayer, for example, can be to welcome the new day, or to reinforce the theme and focus from the previous night, or to set the tone and refocus the group of active teens in preparation for the theme of the new day's talks and direction. Whatever the purpose, let it be reflected in the prayer. I am not a great fan of gathering the retreat group for prayer and then asking who wants to lead the prayer. I choose instead to have a person ready to lead the prayer, a prayer that has been lovingly and thoughtfully prepared especially for that occasion.

Our own creativity is the gift we can use with few limitations in creating a meaningful prayer experience, spiritual exercise, or liturgy for a retreat. Think big. Think outside the box in your planning. Use music, flowers, rocks, leaves, fabric, sand, incense, candles, water, whatever you have available that will touch the senses of the retreatants in planning your services. Your only limitations are your imagination, common sense, and your budget. But you have the inspiration of the Holy Spirit, so your options are limitless!

PLANNING SPIRITUAL EXERCISES

One of the recurring complaints I receive in youth ministry is that the church is a church of and for adults. Too often the kids complain that they feel they are treated only like children of parishioners and not like parishioners themselves. Without getting into a long, heated discussion on the merits of their complaints, I feel that if this is how they perceive their church, then we should try to look at ways to change this perception. A retreat gives us the forum to do so if we are willing to take the time and put in the effort to create meaningful liturgies, spiritual exercises, and prayer services. This step will help you to do that within the context of the retreat.

I see the comments of the youth as their crying out for a deeper, more meaningful relationship with our Lord in the community of the church. Most of the time, the young person doing the complaining doesn't really know that this is what he really wants, so the only way he knows to verbalize his need is through verbalizing his frustrations with the church. A well thought out and planned spiritual exercise will help them fill that need.

My definition of a spiritual exercise is that it is an extended, more focused prayer service; but instead of the service being led by one or two people, the spiritual exercise requires total participation from the group. I have experienced spiritual exercises that have lasted well over an hour. A spiritual exercise can include journaling, silence, guided meditation, prayer walks, healing services, anointing, or affirmations, just to name a few. One of the most powerful experiences I have taken part in is what other churches call an "Altar Call." This is where the retreatants are given the chance to publicly commit their lives to be followers of Jesus and his teachings. An

"Agape" service or other paraliturgical service can also be included under the heading of spiritual exercises.

I am including an adaptation of a spiritual exercise created by Father Bob Miller. I have used the basic model of this exercise in various retreat settings by changing the readings and focus to meet the needs of the group or the theme. I hope you will enjoy it too. We call it the "Rock Service."

The Rock Service

I generally lead this spiritual exercise in a quiet room with candle-light or indirect lighting to set a reflective tone. The setup for this service will vary according to the number of retreatants. A large, clean, empty trash can is placed in the center of the room. Two lines of chairs facing each other should extend from the trash can in all four directions. This will form a cross-like configuration of chairs facing each other with the trash can in the center of the cross. (Your team should have the room and chairs in place when the retreatants walk into the room.) Near the entrance should be boxes of hand-sized rocks.

As the retreatants enter the room in silence have them choose two rocks and take a seat in the cross. Soft instrumental music sets the meditative spirit of prayer. When all are seated, the leader speaks in a slow, soft, reflective tone, but loud enough for all to hear.

❐ *Meditation*

"Peace I leave with you; my peace I give to you.
I do not give to you as the world gives. Do not let your hearts
be troubled, and do not let them be afraid" John 14:27.

God so wants us to live in a state of peace that peace is written about over ninety times in the New Testament. He wants us to live with the gift of peace of mind and heart. We are created to be in relationship with God and to live in peace with each other. But to live in peace we must first let go of the things that enslave us.

Sitting in your chair, I want you to hold a rock in each hand and place your hands on your legs, palms down, and think of the things that keep us from loving God and ourselves. These things are the burdens we carry within us. The burdens of sin, not loving ourselves, loneliness, fear, insecurities, hatred, immorality, and all the things we carry with us that keep us from living a life of peace in our heart and in our mind. As these burdens come to mind, put all these things into the rocks. (Pause for reflection.)

☐ *Stand,* holding the rocks in your palms. In coming together this weekend we have brought with us the cares and burdens of our lives. Some of these burdens we didn't ask for. They are put upon us by life (raise your right arm over your head). Other burdens we had a hand in. They are of our own making (raise your left arm over your head). Some we call misfortune; others we call sins. Let us reflect for a moment in silence not only on those troubles that tire and discourage us, but also on those faults and weaknesses that separate us and keep us from living united in peace. (Pause for reflection, hands still raised.)

☐ *Reach out* to the person sitting across from you and place your hands against the other person's hand holding the rock between you. Living life separated in pieces makes us weary. We want to reach out, to touch, and nourish others, but often our burdens and cares get in the way. We reach but never really touch each other. Our weaknesses and faults keep us from really feeling the warmth and love of others. There is often so much that comes between us and the other people in our lives. (Pause to reflect.)

☐ *Sit down:* Rest the rocks against your own heart. Our burdens and cares keep us from really being in touch with ourselves, with our feelings. We are sometimes troubled, lonely and uncertain. We live with unspoken secrets and hearts hardened with mistrust. We are not free to speak of the love and peace we have for ourselves and for others. How are our hearts burdened? (Pause for reflection.)

☐ *Reading* from Ezekiel 36:24–28: *"I will take you from the nations, and gather you from all the countries, and bring you into your own land. I will sprinkle clean water upon you, and you shall be clean from all your uncleannesses, and from all your idols I will cleanse you. A new heart I will give you, and a new spirit I will put within you; and I will remove from your body the heart of stone and give you a heart of flesh. I will put my spirit within you, and make you follow my statutes and be careful to observe my ordinances. Then you shall live in the land that I gave to your ancestors; and you shall be my people, and I will be your God."*

☐ *Meditation:* Once again resting your arms on your knees with the rocks in your upturned palms, let all the guilt, all the burdens, and all the sins flow into those rocks. (Pause for meditation. Allow enough time for this important reflection.)

☐ *Share quietly* with the person across from you what the rocks symbolize to you.

☐ *Call* the group to silent reflection again when the sharing is ended. Gospel reading: Matthew: 11:28–30: *"Come to me, all you that are weary and are carrying heavy burdens, and I will give you rest. Take my yoke upon you, and learn from me; for I am gentle and humble in heart, and you will find rest for your souls. For my yoke Is easy, and my burden is light."*

☐ *After the reading:*
Lord, we want to be free to live in this world in peace, but you know how easily we get distracted and weary; We want to reach

you and those in our community but our faults and weaknesses keep us from feeling your presence. Our hope and trust are in you love and mercy that touches us.

> *Lord, have mercy* . . . (Response: *Lord, have mercy.*)

Jesus, you taught us to forgive as we want to be forgiven, and to love as you have loved us. So many troubles, so many selfish ways, so many fears come between us. It is so hard to trust and touch each other. Help us to keep trying, help us to forgive and love each other so we can live in peace.

> *Christ, have mercy* . . . (Response: *Christ, have mercy.*)

Lord, you know how hard it is to really be in touch with ourselves: at times we are troubled and lonely and uncertain. Sometimes, it's so hard to live with our unspoken secrets; to forgive ourselves and our hidden faults and fears. Help us to love ourselves as you love us. Free our hearts to move with the Spirit and find our peace in saying, Yes, I'll keep trying; yes, I am loved.

> *Lord, have mercy* . . . (Response: *Lord, have mercy.*)

☐ *The Lord* wants to free us from our burdens. Many of us will carry each other's burdens as we slowly and silently pass the rocks to the center. The last person in the row will drop the rocks into the trash can. (The sound of the rocks dropping into the can is symbolic of the burdens being released)

☐ (*Optional:* Anointing of the palms of our hands)

☐ *Closing prayer:*
Our hands and hearts are at peace and free now to touch and build, to help and love our God, our neighbors, and ourselves. Let us close this moment by offering one another a sign of peace, joyful in the forgiveness promised us in the name of the Father, and of the Son and of the Holy Spirit. (Response: Amen.)

☐ *Share* the sign of peace.

Prayer Partners:

Prayer partners are a staple of most of my retreats, and I include this spiritual exercise on the first night or morning of the retreat. The team member assigned to this exercise places the name of each retreatant in a bag and during a prayer service we ask the retreatants to pick a name out of the bag. We ask them to keep the name a secret, but to pray for that person all through the retreat. The team member assigned to this exercise also is assigned with providing a way for people to communicate their prayers and support to their prayer partner. Most often the team member decorates a paper bag for each retreatant and tapes them on the walls of the conference room to be used as "mailboxes" for prayer partner notes. (Be sure the retreat center allows you to put things on the walls!) Sometimes we have put retreatants' names on half-sheets of poster board giving each retreatant a prayer poster. In either case, extra markers and paper are always available during breaks for the youth to write supportive notes to each other.

The prayer partners often do very thoughtful things for each other, and throughout the weekend they are reminded to pray for their prayer partner. During the weekend a special spiritual bond is created. At the end of the weekend I end this spiritual exercise with a prayer service. We usually gather, standing in a circle. After prayer I say a little about my prayer partner, and then reveal who it is and give him or her a hug. That person then speaks about his/her prayer partner and reveals who it is and gives him/her a hug. It continues through the entire group until all the prayer partners have been revealed. (If two people have each other and the chain stops, I usually ask a team member to begin the chain again.) Once all prayer partners have been revealed, we end with prayer.

Affirmation Circles:

Affirmation Circles are always a high point on retreat if done properly. This exercise should take about ninety minutes for a group of nine people. The purpose of the affirmation circle is to allow each of the small group members to be affirmed by the rest of their small group.

In our society today, it is a much more common experience to put someone down than to build them up. Nothing is more effective in building someone up than having a group of your peers look you in the eyes and tell you how great you are by affirming you, your gifts and talents, and just the person you are. There are two keys to the success of this exercise. One is having the group leaders make mental notes of the good qualities of their group members throughout the weekend in preparation for affirming them later. The second is having good group dynamics and small-group sharing during the weekend so the group members really get to know one another through their sharing.

Here is how the Affirmation Circle exercise works. The director gives a brief talk on building up the body of Christ by building up and affirming each other. Then the small groups are sent off with these instructions: "The purpose of the Affirmation Circle is to affirm the positive gifts, talents, and qualities we have seen or experienced in the other group members. You would want to affirm things like compassion, humor, kindness, love, forgiveness, understanding, creativity, personal strength, and spiritual strength, and expand on these qualities by giving examples from the weekend."

Then the small groups, led by their team leaders, are sent off to isolated locations throughout the retreat centers where they can be undisturbed and undistracted. One group may choose the chapel, another outside, another inside—wherever they feel comfortable. Remembering the essentials for small-group sharing (which you will read about in Step 6), the small-groups will be seated in a circle with one volunteer sitting in the middle of the circle facing a team member. Looking into the eyes of the person sitting in the middle (and maybe holding his or her hands) the team member affirms the person in the middle by telling them all the good they see in them.

It is important that the team member be prepared for this exercise, as they will set the depth, sincerity, and tone of the process for the whole group. After the team member is finished, the person in the middle turns to the next person in the circle and that person looks into their eyes and affirms them. The person in the middle continues the process until everyone in the circle has affirmed them. Once back to the starting team member all of the people in the circle lay hands on the person in the middle and pray for him/her.

Then someone else comes to the middle facing the team member who starts the process all over again. This continues until everyone, including the team member, has had their time in the middle. This exercise can get a little weepy so have plenty of tissues available.

PLANNING LITURGIES

If you plan to include the celebration of Mass on your retreat, the *first thing* you need to do is to *secure a commitment from a priest*. Your first choice might be your parish priest. If so, let him know the dates of the retreat as soon as you have contracted for the weekend. Because the demands of a parish priest are very high on weekends, you will want to get on his calendar as soon as you can. Most parish priests know the advantage of youth retreats and will do what they can to keep some time open for the retreat if you give them plenty of time up front to plan.

If your parish priest is unable to make the weekend, start shopping around early. If you are using a retreat center run by a religious order, they may be willing to assist you. Another option could be to ask at the Catholic high school or college. They may know of a priest who would be available for you. You might also try a hospital chaplain office as another resource, or check with priests in parishes in close proximity to the retreat center.

It would be ideal if you could have a priest with you all weekend to be available to the retreatants for reconciliation or spiritual direction, and to join the youth in their retreat experience. When you ask a priest to join you on the retreat don't just ask if he can come and say Mass, ask how much time he can give to the weekend. Can he be available to sit in on a few of the talks and be a participant in small groups? Will he be available to hear confessions? When, and for how long? Can he stay for a meal or two? It has always been important to me that the retreatants experience our priests as more than just sacramental vending machines, and also get to know the priest in another context. I want them to learn about this man who chose the sacrament of Holy Orders, and why he chose this as his vocation, and what it is like to live and love life as a priest.

Besides the priest who will preside at Mass, your team should include a liturgist. This person needs to know the flow of the Mass well, and understand the elements of the Mass. High-school altar servers or adult parishioners with experience planning liturgies are two sources for this position.

There are two primary ground rules for the liturgist to remember in planning a successful liturgy. First, if it is a weekend retreat and the Mass is on Sunday or fulfills the obligation for Sunday, the readings should be the readings from the Lectionary for that Sunday. If it is not a Mass for a Sunday obligation, then the liturgist is free to select readings that fit with the theme of the retreat. Long before the retreat weekend the liturgist should meet with the priest about the readings and the other plans for the liturgy, so there are no surprises for either the priest or the liturgist on the weekend.

Second, the liturgist should arrange with the priest in advance for the provision of the essentials needed for Mass, including vestments, sacramentary, Lectionary, chalice, hosts, wine, etc. If he requires that you bring these, then plan in advance. This will avoid the awkward situation where both think the other has prepared for the Mass. It is advisable to contact the priest again the week before the retreat, just to re-confirm all the details.

Following is a sample liturgy worksheet in helping plan for the liturgy of the Eucharist. The items in bold are parts of the Mass in which retreatants can take an active and creative part in the celebration. This form should help your retreat liturgist in the planning process and eliminate any gaps in the flow of the liturgy.

SAMPLE LITURGY

LITURGY OF THE WORD:

Introduction and Welcome to the Mass
Opening Song
Greeting
Penitential Rite
Glory to God
Opening Prayer
First Reading
Responsorial Psalm
Second Reading
Alleluia
Gospel
Gospel Interpretation
Homily

LITURGY OF THE EUCHARIST

Profession of Faith—Creed
Prayer of the Faithful
Presentation of the Gifts Procession and Music
Preface
Holy Holy
Eucharistic Prayer
Our Father
Sign of Peace
Lamb of God
Communion—Eucharistic Ministers
Communion Meditation (Silence—Reading—Song—Dance)
Closing Prayer
Final Blessing
Recessional Song

In planning a liturgy, the liturgist should include the four elements listed earlier in this chapter under planning prayer services as part of their preparations. These include:

❐ The Written Word

❐ Music

❐ Location

❐ Environment, lighting, and props

Each of these is extremely important in planning a meaningful and memorable retreat liturgy. Retreatants helping with the liturgy should be given adequate instructions and plenty of preparation time before the celebration of the Mass takes place. Those selected to read, for example, should be given plenty of time to practice proclaiming the Word and to seek help with pronunciation of unfamiliar names, etc.

Once the final eucharistic celebration is planned, a copy of the planning sheet should be given to the celebrant before the weekend so he isn't surprised about a special procession, skit, liturgical dance, or reading. He can plan his parts of the Mass and his homily according to the theme you have planned, and the liturgy will flow smoothly.

Step Four

CREATING GAMES
AND ICEBREAKERS

☐ Icebreakers and Their Purpose

☐ Community Builders:
Why, How, and When to Use Them

☐ Games

IT'S ALL FUN AND GAMES
(Until Someone Gets Touched by the Spirit!)

Don't dismiss this step just because you have plenty of books from Group and Youth Specialty on icebreakers, community builders, and games. All of the books you have are only helpful if you know how to use them in a retreat setting. Again, everything we do on retreat has to have a purpose. I don't use icebreakers, community builders, or games just because I need fillers or feel I have to have them. I use them to fill a specific need.

It's important to point out that I use icebreakers, community builders, and games on all retreats, not just youth retreats. A good friend and volunteer on many of my retreat experiences is an executive with a large healthcare company. He was asked to put together a three-day retreat experience for the executives of five different departments in his company. He used all the elements of the retreat planning process covered in this book. The critiques after the retreat told the story. The top two rated elements of the retreat were the small-group sharing time and the icebreakers and community builders.

You may be wondering "what's the difference between icebreakers, community builders, and games? Aren't they all just games?" The answer is, "Yes . . . and no."

The difference is what you use and how you use it. I use games just for the purpose of having some fun or giving the retreatants a short break to let go a little bit in an intense schedule. I'll explain differences in icebreakers and community builders, followed by a few examples of both, broken down for large groups and small groups. I hope you will try a few of these on your next retreat. I have used most of them for years and they work every time.

ICEBREAKERS AND THEIR PURPOSE

I cebreakers are meant to do exactly as the name implies—break the ice. I don't care how tight you might think your group is, you still need to do some icebreakers. After a long ride to the retreat center where the retreatants are limited to talking to the few people sitting near them, icebreakers start the whole group on equal footing. They also help bring out the introverts in a safe, large-group setting. Icebreakers are also helpful to those kids who are new to the community and enable them to meet people in a playful environment. The objective of icebreakers is to help instill a feeling of ease and comfort in the retreat and group setting.

The big difference in icebreakers is between large-group and small-group icebreakers. Large-group breakers should be fun, upbeat, and get the kids up and moving to meet people. Small-group icebreakers should be fun as well, but restricted to games or activities that the group can do together. The line between the two is very fine, but they both work toward the same goal of building trust and a sense of security with the people they will be sharing over the course of the retreat. The difference between the two is the intensity of the games or activities your choose. Icebreakers are a testing ground and the intensity should be low and fun. Small-group icebreakers should have a little more intensity and require a little more depth and risk in the game or activity.

Here are a few of my tried and true large and small group icebreakers:

Large-Group Icebreakers:

❒ Bingo

❒ Make an Appointment

❒ Picture This

❒ Stand Up If . . .

Small-Group Icebreakers:

❒ What's My Line?

❒ Me!

❒ Who Are We?

❒ Name That Tune

COMMUNITY BUILDERS

Yes, community builders are meant to do exactly as their name implies too—build community. It's hard as a director to direct a retreat or work on a retreat as a team member where there hasn't been enough time spent building community. We plan the retreat experience expecting to work with a community. It doesn't matter if the retreat is for high school teens, young adults, or parish staff members. We expect the group to be a community. The difficulty comes from the retreatants not meeting our expectations because they don't perceive themselves as a cohesive group, but as individuals who all came to the same retreat. When the groups of individuals come together and work together as a community, the job of the director and team becomes much easier. It's far more effective to lead one group than fifty individuals. Take the time to build community, both in large and in small groups. The objective of community builders is to instill a feeling of belonging and unity with the others in the group.

Large-group community builders once again can be a game or activity that gets the group up and meeting others in the group. Here are a few of my favorites:

I Love People Who . . .

The object of this game is to get the kids moving and out of their comfort zone of friends. The game begins with the large group sitting in chairs in one large circle. Ask for one volunteer to stand in the center of the group and remove that person's chair from the circle. The person in the center yells, "I Love People Who . . ." and they finish the sentence any way they want, as long as it references something about the group. Examples are: "People who have blonde hair," "People who are wearing a watch," "People who are in the tenth grade," "People wearing glasses." If you are one of the "people who," you must get out of your chair and move to the empty chair of someone else who is getting up. The person in the center also runs to fill one of the empty chairs. The last person standing moves to the center and the game begins again.

To add a little twist to the fun I have them introduce themselves to the person on each side of them between each "I love people who…" This helps to begin building community.

Move to the Left, Move to the Right

This game begins with everyone sitting in chairs in a large circle. One person stands in the middle and calls out the "move" instructions. Example: If you are wearing shorts, move five chairs to the right. If the chair you move to is occupied, then you have to sit on the lap of the person sitting in the chair. The next move may be seven chairs to the left if you have a driver's license. This game continues and gets real crazy when you have four or five people piled on top of each other on one chair. You choose when the game is over.

This game is another great way to get kids out of their comfort zone and to begin feeling comfortable as part of the community.

Small-group community builders are similar to small group icebreakers. The difference is you "kick it up a notch." We want the small-group community builders to break down the walls of isolation and get the retreatants to go a little deeper in their personal sharing and in what they reveal about themselves. Here are a few of my favorites:

What Do You Expect?

This is a very basic get-acquainted activity that gives the small-group leaders a quick pulse on each of the group members. Each small group should be seated in a circle (Remember the rules for small-group sharing.). The team leader will ask each of the small-group members the question, "What are your expectations for this retreat," or "What do you expect to get out of this retreat?" The team members in the small group should go first to set the example of how this question can be answered, and then move on to the other members of the group.

Pick Five Facts

Give each small group member an identical piece of blank paper and same-color pen. Have each member write five facts they think no one in the group knows about them. Fold the papers in quarters and put them in a bag. Ask for a volunteer to select one piece of paper from the bag and read the five facts out loud to the group and then the volunteer will try to match the facts to the person who wrote them. Repeat until all the papers have been read. The revelations are often humorous, sometimes startling, but always revealing.

Dinner Table

This is one small-group community builder that I have had the most success with of any large- or small-group builder. This exercise gets the retreatants an opportunity to open up and share with their new community about their family dynamics in an unthreatening context. This also gives the team members a glimpse of how openly the retreatants can share their stories and how they interact with members of their family.

You will need plenty of markers and plain paper for this activity. The small group gathers together and the group members are asked to draw their dinner table, and show where each of their family members sits. Next, using the markers they draw lines between family members, showing the usual lines of communication at their table.

A blue line could indicate a cold relationship. A red line could indicate a heated exchange. A green line could indicate a mutual conversation. Even more revealing, a line of little red hearts could indicate a loving exchange while a heavy scribble of black lines could show tension. No lines could represent that those two family members don't talk to each other.

After they complete their drawings, the small-group members each take turns sharing their dining room exercise and what it represents with the rest of the small group.

GAMES

At the beginning of this section I wrote that games are just for fun. I truly believe that we need to plan a few games in the schedule just for fun, but not for filler. The reasons you want to include a few games in your schedule are varied. You might want a game after you come back from a long lunch break or at the beginning of a new day so that everyone is starting once again at the same place, having fun. You might plan a game after what could be a long, intense small-group sharing or prayer activity just to change the pace of intensity. Have a purpose for planning a game and then plan a game that fits that purpose. If you want to change the pace after a long session for example, don't plan a game that involves waiting in a long line. Have something that involves the entire group and have fun.

You probably have plenty of your own games that your group knows and loves. I would like to share my top three small-group games that can be played anytime or anywhere.

Personal Scavenger Hunt

The first is called "Scavenger Hunt." In this game I have a list of items that could be found on a person, in a wallet, a pocket, or in a backpack or purse. Each of these items has a point value. Easily found items like Chapstick or lip-gloss are given a low point value (like five points). More difficult personal possessions like a postcard or a foreign coin are given a high point value (like thirty-five points). Have each small group form a circle and select a "runner." You stand in the center of the room, surrounded by the ring of small-group circles.

You then call out an item from your list and the point value for that item. The first runner who places that item in your hand wins the points for that group. At the end, the group with the most points wins.

Some items on your list can include:

- ☐ Hair brush
- ☐ Ring with a blue stone
- ☐ Sock with a hole in it
- ☐ Candy bar
- ☐ $20 bill
- ☐ Comb
- ☐ Gum Blue belt
- ☐ Rosary
- ☐ $1.46 in exact change
- ☐ Drivers license
- ☐ School ID card
- ☐ Library card
- ☐ Red pen
- ☐ Scrunchy
- ☐ Nail file
- ☐ Picture of a pet
- ☐ Cross on a chain

By the way, students who have been in my program before are wise to the fact that every sock has a hole in it—the one you put your foot into!

The Clothesline

The second game is called "The Clothesline." This game starts at the starting line at one end of the room, and a finish line about twenty to forty feet away, depending on the size of the small groups. Each small group has a place at the starting line. The object of the game is for each small group to connect objects of clothing such as belts, shoe laces, sweaters, jackets, hats, shoes, neck chains, gloves, etc., into a straight line from the starting line to the finish line. The first team to complete the clothesline unbroken from start to finish wins the game.

A word of caution from the voice of experience: You might have to warn overly competitive boys that pants are disqualified from this game and are to remain on at all times.

Holy-wood Squares

"Holy-wood Squares" is patterned after the TV gameshow *Hollywood Squares*. For this game you need nine "squares," two "contestants," and yourself as the host. To set the stage, the first three squares sit on the floor; the next three squares sit in chairs directly behind the first three. Standing behind the three chairs are the third three squares. The two contestants are the "X" and the "O."

The game is played following the rules of the TV show. The contestants take turns choosing a square to answer one of my questions. The contestant can either agree with the square's answer or disagree. If the contestant is right, that square holds up an X or an O, corresponding with the contestant. When a contestant has three squares in a row, they win.

I use this game as a teachable moment, so the questions I ask are usually related to the church or our faith. The categories of questions cover topics such as Sacraments, Liturgy and the Liturgical Year, Church History, Old Testament Scripture, New Testament Scripture, and Saints. Here are a few sample questions:

Q. Who is the patron saint of TV?   (A. St. Clare)

Q. The first pope not born in Italy was who?   (A. St. Peter)

Q. What color vestment does the priest wear
   during advent?   (A. Purple)

Q. Who wrote the first Gospel?   (A. Mark)

Q. The Mass is divided into two parts.
   What is the first part called?   (A. Liturgy of
                                                      the Word.)

Over the years, I have developed over two hundred questions and answers that I take with me on retreats or when I am asked to speak to a group. All of the questions can be worded for a fill-in-the-blank answer, true or false answer, or multiple choice.

Asking church or faith-based questions can only become a teachable moment if you can explain why, for example, the priest wears purple during Advent. Have fun creating your own list of questions. Begin by creating questions that relate to the particular liturgical season you are in, or a subject you are preparing to speak about.

Step Five

CREATING THE SCHEDULE

☐ Retreat Scheduling

☐ Sample Retreat Schedule

☐ The Twenty-One Elements
   of the Retreat

☐ Plan B—What to Do If . . .

RETREAT SCHEDULING

In steps one through four, I outlined the key elements of a retreat: theme, talks, prayer services, spiritual exercises, and games and icebreakers. Now it is time to put them together in an orderly fashion that will lead to a great retreat experience.

In putting a retreat schedule together we strive for balance between the key elements of a retreat. We also need to look for the flow of the retreat. Let's take a look at a scheduling flow problem to illustrate this point. Mass was to take place on Saturday morning of a retreat, a talk on reconciliation was scheduled to take place at the end of the day, and the retreatants were to take turns going to confession all afternoon. It would flow better if the talk on reconciliation was presented before the priest or priests begin hearing confessions, thus preparing the retreatants for Reconciliation. It would also be better to have Mass after Reconciliation instead of before so that more retreatants would be prepared to receive the Eucharist. Now many of you may think this is a "no-brainer" example, but I wouldn't be using it if I hadn't actually seen it on a retreat schedule I was asked to evaluate.

While this example may seem completely obvious, there are countless other retreat activities in the schedule that may not be so evident on first glance. On page 88 is a sample of a schedule of a weekend retreat I directed. I am using a schedule that had the youth traveling to the retreat on a bus. Because I so firmly believe that the retreat begins in the parking lot of the church as the kids arrive, I include in the schedule the team's arrival at the church thirty minutes prior to the arrival of the retreatants.

Please note that this schedule does not include the activities of the retreat team members designated to be in the advance team. I always send an advance team to the retreat site three to four hours before the arrival of the retreatants. Their responsibility is to assign students to dorms, decorate the dining room (if required), set up the sound system and environment of the conference room and chapel, prepare snacks, and be a welcoming committee when the bus arrives.

It is important to personalize the retreat facilities as much as possible to create a warm, welcoming atmosphere. It also heightens the sense of expectation in the retreatants. If special attention is paid to the facilities, they sense that a special retreat experience lies ahead of them. An unspoken sense of security begins as the retreatants wonder, if the team puts that much work into preparing the room, what is the rest of the weekend going to be like for us? *"Look at the birds of the air; they neither sow nor reap nor gather into barns, and yet your heavenly Father feeds them. Are you not of more value than they?"* (Matthew 6:26) The advance team's preparations are a vital component in the group's transition to the retreat center.

One last note before we delve into the retreat schedule itself. As I have written before, attention to detail makes the difference between a retreat and a great retreat experience. You will see that my schedule accounts for every minute of the retreat. Even though I try to follow the schedule as closely as possible, I am not a slave to the schedule. I allow the Holy Spirit to do his work. If we have scheduled thirty minutes for small-group sharing and I sense from the small-group leaders that the sharing is good and that they need more time, I encourage them to continue. I will try to make up the time lost later in the weekend. I make up time by shaving a few minutes off of a break or at a meal. If we have two games planned for after our lunch break, we may do only one. I am selective, however, and never shave the talks, prayer services, sacraments, and other more substantive components of the retreat.

Following is an example of a standard retreat schedule. This basic schedule has worked for me for twenty years, with minor adaptations based on the nature of the retreat. The numbers in parenthesis next to the times listed on the sample schedule correspond to the explanations given for each segment starting on page 93. The talks listed are sample topics.

SAMPLE RETREAT SCHEDULE

FRIDAY:

3:30   (1)   Team arrives at church
(Advance Team already at retreat center)

Set up at church for arrival of retreatants

Greeters: _____

_____

_____

Logistics: _____

_____

Luggage: _____

_____

_____

_____

Bus Captain: _____

_____

4:00   Retreatants arrive at church

4:30   Bus leaves for retreat center
Eat dinner on bus

7:30   (2)   Arrive at retreat center
Unload busses and set up in dorms
Snacks and drinks

8:00 (3) Introduction and orientation
           Welcome
           What is a retreat?
           Expectations, cooperation, and confidentiality
           Rules and regulations (Mark's two rules)
           Introduce team

           Theme and theme song: _____

           Opening Prayer: _____

8:30 (4) Nametags and large-group icebreakers

           _____

           _____

9:15 (5) Break into small groups / Small-group community
           builders

           _____

           _____

10:00 (25) Break

10:10 (6) First talk—"Unity in Community"
           (Team prays over speaker)
      (6a) Silent reflection

10:30 (7) Small-group sharing

10:50 (8) Night Prayer _____

11:05 (9) Bedtime

11:25   Lights Out.

SATURDAY

7:00   Wake-up call

8:00   (15)   Breakfast

8:45   (10)   Team meeting

9:00   (8)   Morning Prayer _____

9:15   (11)   Large-group games _____

                             _____

                             _____

9:45   (12)   Prayer Partners _____

                             _____

10:00 (13)   Small-group games / Community builders

10:15 (15)   Break

10:30 (14)   Second talk—"Respect and Awe of the Lord"
                             (Team prays over speaker)

10:50 (6a)   Reflection

10:55 (7)   Small-group sharing

11:45   Break

12:00 (15)   Lunch, free time

2:30   Gathering _____

                             _____

2:45   (14)   Third talk—"You Try Talking to My Parents!"
              (Team prays over speaker)

3:05   (6a)   Reflection

3:10   (7)   Small-group sharing/Set up for Mass

4:05   Break

4:15   (16)   Spiritual exercise
              (spiritual groups)

5:10   (17)   Mass   _____

              _____

6:15   Dinner   _____*Décor for special dinner?*_____

              _____*Costumes?*_____

7:30   (18)   Skits   _____

              _____

9:25   Break

9:30   (14)   Fourth talk—"Love, Love, Love"
              (Team prays over speaker)

9:55   (6a)   Reflection

10:00 (7)   Sharing

11:00   Parent Letters

11:30 (9)   Bedtime

11:45   Lights Out

SUNDAY:

7:30   Wake-up call

8:30   (15)   Breakfast

9:30   Morning Prayer _____

9:45   (14)   Fifth talk—"Acceptance of Self"
                (Team prays over speakers)

10:10 (19)   Affirmation circles

12:15   Lunch and clean-up

1:30   (14)   Sixth talk—"Wonder about the Future"
                (Team prays over speaker)

2:00   (20)   Summary, Prayer Partners, and Prayer service

                _____

                _____

3:00   Board buses

6:00   (21)   Closing Mass at the church
                (Often followed by potluck at church)

THE TWENTY-ONE ELEMENTS OF THE RETREAT

You may be wondering about the numbers in parenthesis for various parts of the retreat. I will describe and explain each of these activities in the corresponding sections below:

1. *Assembling at the Church*

I like to have the team arrive at the church about thirty minutes before the retreatants arrive. This gives them time to load their stuff on the bus and get set up for the kids.

❏ *Greeters*

I always assign two or three team members the job of greeters. Their task is to welcome the retreatants with a warm, friendly greeting. They are also available to give directions and answer parents' questions. If the student is a little hesitant about the retreat or if the parent has a few fears about sending their child away for the weekend, a good greeter can do wonders in washing away hesitancy and fears. This welcome also shows that the team is ready to serve this weekend. Greeters direct the retreatants where to put their luggage and parents where to bring last-minute paperwork.

❏ *Logistics/Paperwork*

Two to three team members should be assigned to set up a table to help collect any last-minute paperwork. A file will already be prepared for this team, with a folder for each student containing their medical release forms, final payments, love letters from parents, etc. The logistics team checks each file and watches for parents of any students whose file is not complete. They also call parents to remind them to bring any missing paperwork

The logistics team also keeps track of who has arrived and who has not. If we are still missing two or three kids by ten minutes before the bus is scheduled to leave, one member of the logistics team starts making phone calls. This team is responsible to see that all paperwork goes on the bus for the retreat. If there are any individual drivers taking students to the retreat, then a team member must be responsible that a copy of the medical release form is sent along with that driver for each student, and another copy is kept in the primary file.

❐ *Luggage Helpers*

Another two to three team members are assigned to help load the luggage and sleeping bags onto the bus. It is important to emphasize the word help. I don't expect the team to do all the work. Knowing how some kids can get a little flaky, I mean absent-minded, once they get around their friends, luggage helpers insure that all the luggage gets on the bus and we don't end up with a retreatant having to call their parents to deliver their suitcase on Friday night.

The luggage helpers are also responsible to see to it that all supplies are also loaded onto the bus. This may include cases of soda and water, guitars, boxes of markers and paper, and a variety of other materials.

Depending on the individual bus company, your bus driver may assist in loading, or he may just supervise. Be sure to ask what the bus driver prefers.

If you are using individual drivers, the luggage helpers' job is a little more complicated as they direct the loading of each van. Often there might be one or two items left behind, and the luggage helpers are responsible to bring these items to the retreat and find their owners. It is also their responsibility to see that everything has been removed from the luggage compartments before the bus leaves the retreat.

❐ *Bus Captain*

Just prior to boarding the bus, the bus captain will gather the retreatants into a circle and lead them in a prayer for a safe journey. After that, the bus captain is responsible for everything that happens on the bus. This person makes sure that there is a medical release form for each youth on the bus and takes a final head count to match it against the list to be sure no one is left behind. If the bus makes any stops along the way for food, gas, or bathroom breaks, the bus captain is again responsible for this important head count.

The bus captain will remind team members not to all sit together, but to sit in various areas throughout the bus. This helps keep any potentially overexcited kids from getting too rambunctious. Just before arrival at the retreat center the bus captain should circulate a couple of large trash bags through the bus, to collect any trash. Some bus companies charge up to $75.00 extra if the bus driver has to clean out the bus after a messy group.

The bus captain has a copy of a detailed map for the bus driver and a check to pay the driver if that was the contracted arrangement. As long as we are on the topic of the bus, I want to point out once again that the retreat starts on the bus. Keeping this in mind, I ask the team members on the bus to make themselves available to the retreatants, walk up and down the aisles, introduce themselves, engage the lonely ones in conversation, ask others about their school, family, expectations for the weekend, etc. In other words, take this time to do what it takes to make all the kids feel welcomed and loved. Their presence in the aisles also helps keep the noise level down and reduces the chance of a food fight.

The bus captain has similar responsibilities on the way home from the retreat, taking a head count before leaving. It would be a real disaster if the bus got back to the church and you found out that you left a kid at the retreat center because he or she was in the bathroom when the bus left. The bus captain's last duty on the way to and from the retreat is to inspect the bus to see that nothing is left behind.

2. *Arrival at the Retreat Center*

The advance team should have the retreat center ready for the retreatants' arrival. It is always nice if the advance team is holding a welcome banner when the bus arrives. As the luggage helpers assist in unloading the bus, The advance team helps direct retreatants to their dorms, and then to the conference room. The conference room is already set up for the arrival of the retreatants, and snacks and drinks are out. I like to give the kids a little time after their arrival for snacks and to get acquainted with their new surroundings. This free time also lets them run off a little of that energy that was stored up on the bus ride.

3. *Introduction and Orientation*

☐ *Welcome*

During the welcoming address, I introduce myself as the retreat director and explain my role for the weekend. It is very helpful to establish this role for the kids who have never been on retreat before, especially if the last event they were at was a lock-in and they remember me as the winner of the baby food eating competition or being discovered alive at the bottom of a dog-pile at 4:30 in the morning. The role of retreat director is far different and it is important to establish this role for this weekend.

If the retreat center is run by a religious community, I also take a little time to explain the charisms and spirituality of our hosts for the weekend. If the retreat center has a colorful history, like some of the mission retreat centers in California, I give a little history lesson.

This up-front time accomplishes two things for me as the

director. It gives me a chance to talk to the group without being perceived as a threat and it gives me a little time to visually evaluate the temperature of the group. If the group seems to be responding in a positive manner I know I shouldn't have to worry about the behavior of the group this weekend and I can gloss over the rules and regulations. If I have to stop two or three times in the first five minutes to handle a behavior problem, then I know I will have to hammer hard on the rules and regulations.

❐ *What is a Retreat?*

I explain the purpose of the retreat at the beginning of all retreats. I do this for the benefit of the first-time retreatants, as well as a refresher for those who have been on retreat in the past. It also gives me an opportunity to ask those who have been on a retreat before to not play the comparison game. I ask them to hold on to the fond memories of past retreats and to lock them away in their heart-book of memories. I ask them to free their minds to be open to the opportunity for the Holy Spirit to fill new, empty pages in that book with new experiences, growth, and memories.

This is the place in the retreat when I share the analogy of the road trip (found in Step 1 of this book) to help orient them to a retreat in a simple, nonthreatening way.

❐ *Expectations and Cooperation*

I am up front with the retreatants on my expectations of them for the weekend. I talk about their following the rules, cooperating with the schedules, respecting others when they are talking, and respecting confidentiality of the speakers and their small-group members.

I give them a chance to express what expectations they may have of me. This usually catches them off-guard because they don't usually have expectations of a retreat director other than that similar to a teacher, or that I would provide an overall good experience for them. I then tell them what they *should* expect from me this weekend. I tell them they should expect me to respect them and their possessions. They should expect to have a good time, and that this weekend is not going to be a waste of their time. They should expect the team to be prepared and the talks to be informative, and that they should expect us all, as a team, to respect their confidentiality.

If any team members are parents of a retreatant, I tell them that for this weekend they are not parent and child, but team member and retreatant, and to respect each other in those roles.

I end by asking them to change their expectations if they think the food is going to be home-cooked or delivered by the local pizza store. Then I invite them to talk to me if at any time their expectations are not being met. I will do all I can to adjust my part in the weekend to meet these expectations.

I then tell them, as they are free to talk to me about not meeting their expectations, that I will in turn talk to them if I feel they are not meeting my expectations of them. This open show of respect and responsibility gives a positive foundation for expectations and cooperation on the weekend.

☐ *Rules and Regulations*

I believe in setting clear and firm guidelines for the retreatants. I don't believe in giving threats or consequences with each rule. I also don't believe in giving more rules than they need at the time. Friday night's rules and regulations should cover the minimum amount of rules to get through the weekend.

I give the parameters of the retreat center itself, what is allowed and what is not, and what areas can be used and what areas cannot.

I give the rules for small-group sharing before the first small-group sharing session. I give the rules for dorm behavior just before they go to bed. I give the rules for meals and cleanup of the dining hall just before the meal.

Don't downplay the need for rules and regulations, but don't give them more than they need at the time. If you try to explain all the rules at one time they get tuned off, but if you give two or three directions as needed, it makes you the director look less like a dictator and more like a guardian.

I always try to end rules and regulations with "Mark's two rules":

Rule 1: Control your hormones.

Rule 2: Don't embarrass Mark.

The kids in my youth group quickly come to understand that these two rules cover just about everything. "Control your hormones" is self-explanatory. The second rule acknowledges that as the retreatants' representative to the people who run the retreat center and the bus company, and to the parish and the community, I am responsible and answer for my youth group's actions. Rule number 2 basically asks the youth to act in a manner that will never cause me embarrassment.

❒ *Team Introduction*

Even if the retreatants are familiar with some of the team members, always take the time to introduce each member of the team. If you have any short, fun, personal stories you think would be appropriate to share about the team members, I encourage you to share them (with their prior permission) as a way to enhance the introduction.

❒ *Theme and Theme Song*

A good, clear explanation of the theme of the retreat is necessary to help set the tone for the retreat. Part of the introduction can include the process you and the team went through to pick the topic and why you chose it. If you have a song to go with the theme, the choice to play it before or after the introduction (or both) is up to you. The most important thing is that the song is selected to enhance the theme of the retreat, and not just because your musicians know how to play it or because it is popular at the time.

❏ *Opening Prayer*

As with all prayer services, the opening prayer should have a clear purpose and be well planned. The opening prayer marks the spiritual beginning of the retreat. It should include the Lord's blessings for the team, retreatants, activities, and the presenters of talks. The prayer should give thanks for God's hand in selecting the retreatants and team for this unique weekend. It could also include the parish community and family members back home who are praying for the success of this retreat experience. If you have a spiritual or theme environment, the prayer can be focused around that environment. If you are using a candle to symbolize the presence of Christ at the retreat, this is a good time to light the Christ candle. The prayer should invoke the presence of the Holy Spirit to move mightily upon the weekend.

Friday night of a retreat can be a busy time, but I include all of the aforementioned elements in the introduction and orientation of each retreat in order to lay a firm foundation on which the rest of the retreat will build. I may change the order to emphasize different elements depending on the group, the circumstances, and the creativity of the team. I encourage you to be creative and listen to the Holy Spirit.

4. *Large-Group Icebreakers*

If you are not clear on the difference between icebreakers and community builders, please refer back to Step 4. Two to three icebreakers are appropriate at this point of the retreat. These icebreakers give the kids a chance to move around and have some fun after sitting for a while. It also gives the adult team members a chance to get acquainted with the group and let go of any fears they might have. The activities have been prepared well in advance by those assigned to the task, and they have assembled any materials that will be needed. Those assigned to the icebreakers will lead the activities. Often the result of one of the activities is the creation of nametags that the retreatants and team members wear throughout the weekend.

5. *Small-Group Activities*

Breaking the retreatants and team into small groups can be more than just reading names from a list and telling each group where to assemble. Be creative and make it a game or activity, as long as they have a little fun and end up with the group to which they have been assigned. Some retreatants will want to be in the same small group as their friends. If they end up in a group as a result of a game (even though the team has predetermined how the game will divide the kids) it feels "fair" to the student.

Once they are in small groups, "community builders" become very important. The first community builder should be chosen to reveal as much information about the retreatant as possible without being threatening. Any variety of the "What Do You Expect" exercise in Step 4 is a good one to use here. After allowing ample time for sharing, I usually follow that with the "Dinner Table" exercise, again found in Step 4. Once the groups complete this exercise, I ask them to pick a name for their group and instruct them to make up a cheer, song, or short skit that they can use to introduce themselves to the other groups. It's a good idea to put a time limit on this activity; experience tells me that they will take all night creating very elaborate presentations.

If done properly, these activities start to break down the walls of individuality and replace them with the bonds of community. The first two community builders should give the group facilitators a great deal of information about the people in their group, including their interests, self-image, and family systems. The third activity is designed to give the group its first opportunity to work together and to form an identity as a group. It also helps the facilitators zero in on the personalities of the individuals in the group, as well as give the director a sense of the personality of each group.

Again, I want to emphasize that everything I do on the retreat has a purpose. It's your job as director to make it look like fun.

Now, sit back and relax. I want to tell you another story. No, don't close your eyes . . . you're reading! On one retreat the bus was involved in a minor accident. Nothing big, thank God, just a bent fender. Without going into detail about the investigation and paperwork involved, the bus was over two hours late and the kids were off the wall. I made the decision to drop most of elements 3, 4, and 5 from the schedule. We played games for a while to allow the kids to get rid of the anxiety and pent-up energy after sitting on a bus for close to four hours. After the games we had our first talk and I was back on schedule.

By Saturday afternoon I had heard from most of the team that something was wrong. The retreat wasn't working, the groups weren't working, and the retreatants didn't seem to be "getting it"—they lacked the sense of community they usually had by this time of the retreat.

During the break, I took a walk with Mary Jo, the assistant director, to pray and evaluate the problem. The only difference we found between this retreat and previous retreats was the changes I made Friday night. We decided to call a quick team meeting and ask their input on changing the retreat schedule for the next few hours of the afternoon, to include all of the elements I had cut out the night before. They all agreed and in fact encouraged it. We made the adjustment and by bedtime Saturday night at the team meeting all agreed that the retreat was back on track and community was building.

The purpose for sharing this story is to reemphasize the importance of all the elements in this process. It also reflects the importance of the willingness and flexibility of a qualified team to allow the Holy Spirit to work.

6. *Presentations*

The first talk helps set the pace for the weekend. It lets the retreatants experience that the schedule is balanced between fun activities, and powerful presentations. The first talk shouldn't be too heavy with a great deal of personal testimony. It should cover one of the four specific areas covered in Step 2: Spiritual, Personal, Relational, and Communal. It could incorporate personal reflections about the theme of the retreat, or be used to lay out a foundation for the rest of the presentations. Whatever you choose to use for the first talk, it should be given on the first night of the retreat. Remember, that first night lays the foundation for the rest of the weekend, and we don't want to send the kids to bed thinking it's all, just games and icebreakers. It's better to give them something solid to think about before they go to bed.

❒ *Reflection*

At the end of each talk, I allow a few minutes for silent reflection. This gives the kids some time to personalize and reflect on what they have heard, before they go into small-group discussion. This is usually accompanied with a tape or CD of a song or music chosen by the speaker to reinforce the message of the talk, or by soft instrumental music conducive to meditation and reflection.

7. *Small-Group Sharing*

After every talk we break into our assigned small groups for discussion. To facilitate this discussion, the presenter of the talk gives each group a written list of reflective questions (prepared in advance) about the subject of the talk. The small-group facilitator leads the group in this sharing. It isn't as important to get through all the questions as it is to encourage all the group members to share. They don't have to follow the progression of the questions as they are written. They may decide that by the level of sharing during the first question they should move to the third question next, instead of the second. As director, I have trained and empowered the facilitators to do what they think is best for their group. The only thing I insist upon is that they stay on topic and don't let the discussion wander, and that they encourage everyone to share.

For control of noise level and to provide for more intimacy, I encourage the group leaders that at least some of them find another place for small-group sharing other than the conference room. Some choose a corner of the chapel, an area in the dining room, the floor in a dorm, or if its good weather, they may go outside and sit under a tree (usually not at night). I only ask that they let me know where they are going so I will know where to find them if they are late.

8. Night Prayers

Night prayer puts closure on the day. This should be a quiet, calming prayer time, possibly accompanied by a soft song or calming music. It helps bring the evening to a peaceful end, and it helps bring the group down before bedtime.

9. Bedtime

I don't know of a youth minister who sends his or her group to bed and expects them to all be tucked in and quiet when the lights go out. This may be our plan, but we all know its not part of the kids' agenda. That's why it's important to cover the bedtime expectations ahead of time, and to discuss the team's role in expediting these expectations at a team meeting.

After night prayers, the group is usually settled down, and it is then that I take the opportunity to speak to them about my expectations and rules for bedtime. I talk about the sacrifices needed to live and sleep in community. I explain about the need for some people to get seven or eight hours of sleep a night. I explain about some people being night people and some people being morning people, and that no matter what your personal style is, we must all respect the needs of the community, not self. I would like to be able to tell you I have a 100-percent success rate. If I did, you'd probably close this book and say this guy is dillusional and needs treatment. What I can honestly say, is I have about a 90-percent success rate with the lights out and quiet within an hour of sending them to bed. This may be thirty minutes later than I hope for, but I have to remember it's youth ministry, and I am going to be challenged. It's part of the job.

As important as it is to the good of the community to get the lights out and the dorms quiet at a decent hour, it is equally important that no one gets up at 4:00 A.M. to start the showers and blow dryers, waking the rest of the dorm. I instruct the group that except for going to the bathroom, they must remain quiet and in bed until wake-up call.

10. Team Meetings

I try to have two or three short meetings with the team throughout the weekend. The team are my eyes and ears in small groups and can gauge the temperature of the weekend better than I can by myself. I ask them if there is anything I need to know about their small group or any particular retreatant. I ask if there is anything they feel the retreat needs so far. I believe that the team is responsible for the retreatants, and I am responsible for the team. With this in mind, I ask if there is anything they need or I can do for them. I review the schedule of events for the next day or for the rest of the day, and we close in prayer. After the team meeting it is my responsibility to follow up on any suggestions or needs that have been brought to my attention.

11. Large-Group Games

After morning prayer we start with large group games. This helps recapture part of the momentum built last night, but lost because of the break for sleep.

12. Prayer Partners

Prayer partners are covered in Step 4 under Spiritual Exercises. I usually include it in Friday night's activities, however, in this particular schedule I include it as part of the Saturday morning activities. Prayer partners take time to develop, so if you plan to include them

on your retreat, do not schedule it to begin any later than early
Saturday morning.

13. Small-Group Game / Community Builder

This is more a rebuilder and enhancer than just a builder. As with
the large-group game, the purpose is to rebuild or reestablish the
sense of community created the night before, but was lost because of
the need for rest. A game or activity can be used here as long as all
the group members are participating. Competition between groups
can contribute as a rebuilder of group spirit at this point.

14. Presentations

The first talk already set the foundation on which all the rest of the
talks will build. Now, the intensity of the presentations grows with
the progression of the schedule. The Saturday night talk is usually
the crescendo, with Sunday's talks preparing the retreatants to return
home on Sunday afternoon. The last presentation on Sunday is used
to recap and put closure to the weekend. The talk can include some
personal reflection but should deal more with closure and preparing
the retreatants to return to home and school without losing the Spirit,
and to go forth and spread this Spirit in their own communities.

15. Meals, Free Time, and Breaks

Plenty of time should be given at mealtime to relax or play after the
meal. This is usually about thirty minutes max, except after lunch on
Saturday. The extra free time after lunch is as good for the team as
it is for the retreatants. Saturday is a very long day, and the kids
need to run, play, and get all that energy out. They also like to take
this time to explore the retreat center grounds and relax. At the
same time, the adults who were up late the night before need time
to rest (. . . at least this adult does!).

It's also important to schedule plenty of short breaks throughout
the retreat. You will see from the schedule that I plan breaks at

natural transition points; usually after a small-group sharing or before a talk. Experience tells me that no matter how much free time or breaks are given, kids are kids, and according to them it's never enough. If you have a balance in your youth ministry program between social and spiritual events, most of the kids will be able to deal with the free time offered in the schedule.

16. *Spiritual Exercises and (17.) Liturgies*

Spiritual exercises are covered in Step 3. Again, they should be created to add to the flow of the weekend. For example, the spiritual exercise chosen for one particular retreat dealt with forgiveness and reconciliation. This was created as a natural flow from the talk on parents, and flowed into the Mass. The readings selected for the liturgy of the word dealt with forgiveness, and because the presider was informed of the day's events and activities well in advance, he was able to pull it all together in his homily, without repeating what was covered in the talk or the spiritual exercise. He was also able to make reference to the talk and the spiritual exercise to make a point in his homily. I find that if I clearly discuss the key elements of the retreat before the retreat, the priest is willing to do whatever he can to enhance the spiritual exercise. The key is to be able to clearly verbalize your expectations long before the retreat so it gives them time to prepare. This will help guarantee that your spiritual exercises and liturgies build on each other and on the rest of the retreat, creating a seamless flow in the retreat experience.

18. *Skits*

Another key element to the success of the retreat from a teenager's perspective is laughter and great, creative fun. Skits are the most effective way I have found to let the kids have great fun, be creative, and kind of stay on track as far as the content of the retreat is concerned. My first guideline for the skits is that they must use all the members of the group in performing the skit. Second, the skit must be appropriate and not offensive. Finally, it has to do with something from the retreat so far. For example, they can act out something having to do with the theme, or something covered in one of the talks. Maybe they will act out one of the readings from a liturgy or prayer service. I have even seen them use something from the homily. (Father was more surprised that they had even listened to him than he was that they used his concept in a skit.)

Prior to the weekend the team is aware that skits are included in the schedule. This allows them to make mental notes throughout the day. If the retreatants in their group are having trouble coming up with ideas, the team members can help get the creative juices flowing when the time comes, but may not discuss or even mention skits with their small group until it comes up in the schedule.

I usually bring bags of props for the skits (a variety of hats, belts, robes, shoes, wigs, ties, etc.) I have found that the older, funkier and more colorful the props, the better. These are usually items that I have collected from garage sales, Salvation Army or St. Vincent de Paul stores, or thrift shops. Most of the time I am not looking for anything specific, but if I spot something and my mind says, "You could have fun with that!" I buy it.

It's amazing to see the creativity that results from the group effort and friendly competition between groups. Although we don't judge the skits, I often tell them they get extra points in my book if they can include the retreat director in the skit without using him personally or embarrassing him. This invitation always adds an interesting wrinkle to the skit. Of course, my overall reaction heightens the frivolity of the evening. The performance of each skit always interprets an important point, usually in an atmosphere of side-splitting laughter, and allows the youth to experience the natural high that flows from a vibrant Christian community.

19. *Affirmation Circles*

Affirmation circles are covered in Step 3 under Spiritual Exercises. Affirmation circles always fall near the end of the retreat to allow plenty of time for the group members and team to get to know and appreciate the uniqueness of each person in the group. The talk before affirmations should set the stage for the affirmations. The talks may be a little different from one retreat to another, but I believe so strongly in the need to be confirmed by their peers that I always include affirmation circles in a weekend retreat.

20. Closing Exercises

Just as I believe that the retreat begins at the church and includes the bus ride, I believe the retreat ends at the church as well. It is good, however, to have a closing talk at the retreat center to put closure on the weekend for the retreatants. The closing service can include a special prayer service, anointing individuals, blessings of all the retreatants by the director and/or by the team, etc. If you have a special gift or memento for them as a remembrance of the weekend, this can be included here. As an idea, I have given each of the retreatants a cross to hang in their rooms, or a necklace with the Christ symbol on it, or a candle as a symbol that they are called to be the light of Christ to the world. The closing talk often encapsulates the main points made during the weekend, and includes some of the spontaneous moments and moments when the Spirit touched the group. We also take time at the end of the retreat to reveal prayer partners.

21. Closing Mass at Church

In Step 5, I reviewed details about including families and parish community in the retreat. Having a closing Mass at the parish when the bus returns is great for this, especially if the parish already has a Sunday evening liturgy scheduled. With a good support group in the parish, the church can be decorated with special banners to welcome the kids back. The team and retreatants should have a section in the front of the church reserved for them. The retreatants can be included in the entrance procession, and usually come in smiling and holding hands or arm in arm. The reaction to this from the parents and community is heartwarming. We also include the retreatants in as many parts of the Mass as we can, allowing them to be ushers, musicians, lectors, altar servers, offering prayers of the faithful, etc.

A highlight of the liturgy comes from the support of the pastor. After the gospel, the presider speaks a few words to the retreatants and then invites the youth to come forward and share a little about their weekend.

The youth can be a little hesitant at first, so I prime the pump a little. Before we leave the retreat center I ask a few of the more outgoing kids or those who have been on retreat before to be ready to get up and share a little if Father extends the invitation. Once one or two go up and through their tears and laughter share a story or a poignant moment from the retreat, the floodgates are open and many find they have something to share. The comments can be priceless, especially to the parents and families. "It was like a God bomb went off this weekend, and we got all the fallout." "I always knew I had the light of Christ in me, and finally this weekend the light was lit." The benefits of allowing the community to witness the joy and growth that result from the youth retreats is a great benefit to the parish, the families, and to the youth ministry program.

I offer this one caution, however; allowing the youth to speak at Mass can cause the liturgy to run fifteen or twenty minutes longer than usual. A few days after one of these closing Masses, my pastor told me that he got a couple of complaints about the Mass running long. He asked me if in the future I would put a comment in the bulletin a few weeks before the next retreat, warning the parish that the kids would be returning from a retreat and the Mass may be a little long. I did what he asked (kind of): Starting four weeks before the retreat, I put announcements in the bulletin inviting parishioners to attend the 5:30 Mass, because the youth group will be returning from retreat and they wouldn't want to miss their sharing. Because of that sharing, I added, the Mass may run a little long. The church was packed to the rafters with people of all ages wanting to share in this special liturgical celebration.

PLAN B—WHAT TO DO IF . . .

I always bring extra activities on retreat just in case I need them. What would you do if the ceiling in the conference room leaks, or the hour's worth of outside games you planned has to be canceled due to rain? What if your priest calls and will be an hour late for Mass, which will now interfere with dinner time, or worse yet, what if he's not able to contact you to tell you he will be late? What if dinner will be late? What if one of your presenters gets sick and can't give their talk? What if a retreatant gets sick or injured?

All of these scenarios have happened to me at one time or another, and believe me when I tell you to expect the unexpected. It is your responsibility as retreat director to always have Plan B in your back pocket. I know from experience that having a group of teenagers sitting for even a short period of time with no direction is a recipe for chaos. Here are some of my recommendations. I never left for a retreat without having a folder with the following items:

- ☐ Two additional large-group activities,
  (Bring materials if any are needed.)

- ☐ Two additional small-group activities.
  (Again, bring any supplies you will need.)

- ☐ An outline for a reconciliation service.

- ☐ An outline for an additional spiritual exercise.

- ☐ An outline for a talk.
  (The topic for this talk was usually "Hearing God's Call."
  This topic is easily adaptable to most retreat situations.)

❑ The phone numbers of two or three reliable (and good natured) people from the parish I can call on in case of an emergency.

Chances are you won't have any of these problems on your retreat, but on something as important as a retreat, why leave anything to chance? Having already made plans for as many of these contingencies as possible, and knowing that you have alternative activities with you, with materials all ready to go, will give you peace of mind and allow for a smooth transition if you need to use them. When I have been prepared and needed to use my backup plan, the retreatants often never knew the difference. They never knew that my Plan B wasn't their Plan A all along. A director who is prepared allows for a seamless retreat experience for the youths rather than leaving them disappointed, wondering what might have been.

IN CLOSING . . .

In closing this step, I have one last thing for you to do, and that is to schedule time for your own well-being after the retreat. When I get home after a retreat, my wife has a special dinner waiting for me with a chilled bottle of my favorite Italian water. During dinner my wife and children listen to all my stories and reflections. This time was greatly needed and appreciated. I want to encourage you to surround yourself with friends and loved ones who will let you deprogram after a retreat.

My final suggestion is that you take a couple of days off before you go back to the office. I know you have so much to do that you probably think you just can't take a few days off. I used to tell myself that stuff too, but if I hadn't learned to take care of myself, I would never have lasted over twenty years in youth ministry.

CREATING SMALL GROUPS

☐ Essentials of Creating
the Small Group

☐ Small-Group Facilitating

☐ Listening Skills

ESSENTIALS OF CREATING THE SMALL GROUP

S mall groups play an important part in the process of the retreat. When planned and implemented properly, the experience of community that is created in small groups can carry over far after the retreat, to the large group at youth group meetings. Unfortunately today, the success of gangs in our cities can be directly related to the need for its members to belong to something. The need for this sense of belonging is so strong that it will cause a fifteen-year-old boy to kill another child just to prove he is worthy to belong in the gang.

If we can fill the need for belonging for our youth in small groups on retreat, then the youth will want to continue to belong to the community at large, and will stay active in their youth ministry program after the retreat experience.

Two important things in creating your small groups are size and mix. Creating small groups should never be done by chance or at the last minute. Names should not be randomly drawn from a hat. The team should play an active role in breaking the retreatants into small groups. The retreat segment of my youth ministry program has been so successful that all forty-eight available spaces for retreatants are usually filled within ten days of mailing out the applications (eight weeks before the retreat). I have included a copy of my standard retreat application in Step 9. You will see that it includes a series of questions. The retreatants' answers to these questions are invaluable in selecting small groups.

At a team meeting about two weeks prior to the retreat, the team decides who will be in each group. I include the team in this process because it's impossible for me to know all the little characteristics of each applicant. Having youth-group members on the team comes in handy during the task. In many cases they have known many of the kids for years, and have insights into their relationships and current situations that I could never know. Many of the adults on the team have knowledge that is also helpful in this process.

So, here we sit at team meeting with forty-eight applications and the task of dividing them into small groups. Where do we start? The following list defines the criteria I use in creating the small-group mix:

- ☐ Keep a balance in the group of boys and girls.

- ☐ If your program includes kids from different high schools (I once had a group that drew from six schools!) try not to overload any group with too many kids from one high school.

- ☐ Divide older (eleventh and twelfth grade) students among all the groups. This helps with having experienced retreatants with younger students. Their age and experience helps set the tone in the group, and can be an unspoken prompt to the younger students to behave in a more mature fashion. Retreatants also gain much from the sharing of younger and older members, in learning how the Lord works in their everyday life.

- ☐ Do not put best friends together in the same group. This also goes for boyfriends and girlfriends. (Need I say more?)

- ☐ Separate siblings. Additionally, if you have a parent of a retreatant on the team, do not put the parent and child in the same group. The child will speak more freely in a group that does not include his or her parent.

❏ Keep personalities in mind. Try to keep a balance in the groups between introverts and extroverts. Your team will appreciate this!

❏ You may have a retreatant who you perceive may have a problem in small groups, whether due to behavioral problems or due to a unique situation in that child's life (recent death in the family, etc.). If so, make sure you put that person in a group with an adult team leader with retreat experience, and who you think has the perception and sensitivity to work with that person.

❏ The size of your group depends on the number of team members and retreatants you have. As a rule of thumb, I would never have a group larger than nine people, including the team members.

❏ The ratio of team members to youth will vary according to the size of the group. I would never assign more than five retreatants to one team member (for a total group size of six). My larger groups of nine would include two team members facilitating a group of seven retreatants. Groups larger than a total of nine would find it very hard for each person to have adequate time to share in a given time period. Groups smaller than six might have a limited variety of sharing, which limits the variety and dimensions of faith that are imparted to the group members.

❏ Team members will offer additional criteria for selection of small groups, based on their knowledge of the retreatants.

❏ I usually assign two team members to each group, even if one of the groups is small. If one team member gets sick during retreat, there is another member to facilitate the group. Each group usually has one team member who is an adult, and one who is a youth group member with previous retreat experience. This balance in leadership has proved to be most effective over the years. The adult might be more of a parent or mentor figure to the group, while the youth leader is a model and peer to the group members.

If you have any past experience with any of the retreatants or if you are aware of any medical problems, share this information privately and confidentially with that person's small-group leader. When sharing this information, do not make a judgment statement, just stick with the facts.

For example, if you have a boy in the group who plays the drums in the school band, you know that he tends to carry a tune in his head, and without thinking, beats out the rhythm on everything and anything around him. This was the case with my son, Mark. I mentioned to his small-group leader that Mark is a drummer and his hands are always tapping a tune. I offered that if the adult sits near to (but not always next to) Mark, he can quietly reach over and gently calm one hand and Mark will get the signal. Now the group leader knows what to expect from Mark without labeling him a problem. The group leader's perception would have been different if I had just said that Mark frequently breaks the flow of discussions by beating on his chest and thighs.

In another example, I once had a student with Turret's Syndrome in my program. Once again, I spoke privately and confidentially with his small-group leader about his condition, and what to do if he should have an episode.

I find it helpful to make group leaders aware of any changes in the retreatants' home or school life. These would include situations where a student has just moved to the community, parents recently divorced or separated, a death in the family, or recent changes in schools. They might also need to know if there is substance abuse or conditions such as ADHD that might effect behavior. In all instances, the emphasis is never on a trouble-maker kid, but on a potentially troubled kid. The reason for disclosure in confidence is never for the sake of gossip, but for the sake of enhancing the potential that this child will have a successful retreat experience, and that they will allow the others to enjoy the same.

Just as I am responsible for the team and the team is responsible for the retreatants, I designate which team members will be paired together as small-group leaders and facilitators. Then, according to the above criteria and the additional information gained from the applications, the team prays over the retreat applications and begins grouping them in separate stacks, switching back and forth until they agree on the balance of each group. Once groups have been assigned, they remain so throughout the retreat. The only exception is when a retreatant cancels and the next person on the waiting list joins. This new person is not automatically "plugged in" to the vacated position in the small group. We use a much shorter discernment process to adjust the groups for the addition of this person.

With the importance that small-group sharing plays in the internal processing of the weekend by each student, creating small groups should never be left to chance; it should be afforded the attention and time to assure that these groups will be as balanced as possible to ensure the success of the retreat.

SMALL-GROUP FACILITATING

If a retreat was a meal, the presentations would be the meat; what happens in the small groups, the potatoes; and everything else, the appetizers, side dishes, and dessert. The purpose of the talks and the presenters' examples and witness is to encourage the retreatants to look at their own lives and journey and see where they can change and grow. The time spent in silence after a talk should allow the retreatant a safe environment to transfer the speaker's information into how it applies to their life journey. The time spent in small groups allows the retreatants to express their reflections and how the information applies to themselves, and to hear how others respond to the same topics.

After the presentation and the silent reflection that follows, the speaker provides a set of questions to each small-group facilitator. Once the retreatants gather into small groups, the group members are asked the sharing questions to help each member verbalize their reflections in a safe environment. To enhance this sharing I often provide journals to the retreatants to write down their thoughts during the silent time after the talk.

A well-trained small-group facilitator provides a safe environment for this reflection and sharing to happen. Fear prevents the freedom to share from the heart, but in a safe environment, fear is extinguished. We want the retreatants to feel free to be themselves and to share their feelings without being judged. They need a fully positive personal relationship and environment based on trust, freedom, acceptance, and confidentiality.

The facilitator's role is to provide this type of environment for this level of sharing to occur. The facilitator creates this atmosphere by sharing from the heart, and then by not judging, evaluating, interrupting, or criticizing the retreatants' sharing. The facilitator should also be a model for the group in attitude, posture, mannerisms, and words. They will be encouraging and affirming listeners by their body language and eye contact.

This may seem simple, but it doesn't necessarily come naturally. Let's look at some ways we can help the facilitator achieve this level of small-group sharing. Listed below are a few of the do's and don'ts for small-group facilitators. Get to know them well and go over them in detail with your team during one of the team meetings before the retreat. You might want to review them again at one of the first team meetings during the retreat.

DO's

- ☐ Do stick to the topic.
- ☐ Do accept people for who they are.
- ☐ Do smile, nod your head, etc.
- ☐ Do look the person sharing in the eye.
- ☐ Do share of yourself.
- ☐ Do trust in the Lord.
- ☐ Do let a person finish speaking.
- ☐ Do make people feel accepted.
- ☐ Do sit in an attentive and affirming posture and encourage retreatants to do the same.
- ☐ Do thank the retreatants for sharing with the rest of the group.
- ☐ Do give everyone a chance to share.

DON'Ts

☐ Do Not stray from the topic.

☐ Do Not judge.

☐ Do Not be critical.

☐ Do Not let your attention wander.

☐ Do Not lecture or teach.

☐ Do Not count on self.

☐ Do Not interrupt

☐ Do Not probe.

☐ Do Not shuffle too much or let the retreatants get up and stretch.

☐ Do Not allow anyone to talk too much and take time away from the others.

☐ Do Not leave anyone out.

In small-group sharing, we hope to peel back a few layers to get closer to the core of the retreatants' lives and relationships. Small-group facilitators should understand that when someone shares they offer to each other something belonging to them as an individual. When they share what they feel, they are building a confidence and a trust with each other. It is natural to feel a certain sense of risk as they do this, but this sense of risk can be overcome by the reassurance that is given by the people in the group. It is most helpful to know that this sharing is sacred and that anything shared within the group will be kept confidential. The facilitators should understand that:

- ❐ Sharing is a time to speak from our hearts and a time to listen with our hearts.

- ❐ Sharing is a time to tune ourselves in to the others as they share with us.

- ❐ Sharing is not a time to teach anyone else anything.

- ❐ Sharing time is not a time to share about anyone else—just yourself.

- ❐ Sharing is not a time to judge anyone else or even help anyone else.

- ❐ Sharing time is not a time to solve problems. If anyone has a problem that needs to be discussed, there are other times to do this. Do not use sharing time.

LISTENING SKILLS

One of the most important characteristics of effective small-group facilitators is that of being a good listener. To understand what good listening skills are, it is helpful to know what they are not. Perhaps you have experienced these on many occasions:

☐ Preoccupation with what's on their own mind.

☐ Poor eye contact and/or blank facial expressions.

☐ Distracted by other people and things in the room.

☐ Cuts in to finish the speakers' thoughts for them.

☐ Jumps in too quickly if the speaker hesitates, without allowing the speaker to finish thoughts.

☐ Tunes out speaker because of speaker's tone or language.

☐ Discounts speaker's sharing by telling their own similar but more exaggerated story.

☐ Goes on to next speaker without acknowledging previous speaker's sharing.

☐ Listens to words, but ignores body language, facial expressions and tone.

There is a multitude of books and advice on good listening skills. My favorite is *The Art of Christian Listening* by Thomas N. Hart (Paulist Press, 1981). The point is that if we want the retreatants to be open and responsive during the retreat, then the team needs to be prepared to tune themselves out and tune in to the retreatants, picking up not only their words, but their feelings, body language, and their issues.

One final word on small-group facilitating regards the posture of the group. For effective group dynamics it is important during small group sharing that the group facilitator has all members of the group seated physically at the same level and prominence in the group. This means that if the group is sitting on the floor, everyone in the group is sitting on the floor. Don't allow someone to sit on the edge of a sofa or in a chair.

Psychologically, allowing that to happen gives that person dominance over the group. The reverse, allowing someone to lie down while the rest of the group is sitting up, gives that person the power to break the energy in a group. Allowing someone to sit at the same level but just outside the group's circle has the same effect. If a member has a handicap, try to position the group so that everyone else is on the same level. For functions of sharing, my groups usually don't use tables, but opt for the more open circle of chairs or, more often, for the floor. In my experience this has produced more intimate groups.

Don't get me wrong here. I'm not saying that we want to control the retreatants. What we want to control is the environment in small groups to allow for the best quality of sharing possible.

Step Seven
CREATING THE PRESENTATIONS

☐ Preparing a Presentation

☐ Critiquing Presentations
at Team Meetings

PREPARING A PRESENTATION

S ince the retreat team is responsible for the retreatants, during early retreat preparation team meetings, the team picks a theme, reviews the retreatants' applications for their concerns and interests, and selects presentation topics that would be appropriate to the theme and to the group. As director, I am responsible for the team, so I assign the talks to my team members. As you will see later, each presenter is required to give their talk to the rest of the team in later team meetings as preparation for the retreat, and the team has the opportunity to critique the talk and offer comments and suggestions.

This isn't going to be a speech-writing class. I will leave that to Toastmasters. But over the years I have listened to hundreds of retreat talks, (some talks I have heard three or four times!) and I have observed a variety of styles in preparation and delivery. Because this isn't a speech-writing class, I want to focus on what I think is most important, and that is scope, focus, and target. After we look at preparation and how to write a presentation, we will look at scope, focus, and target.

Preparation

When team members who are assigned to give a talk on the retreat come to me for help and direction on composing their talk, the first thing I ask is if they have prayed to God for inspiration yet. If the answer is no, I immediately join them in prayer. I am a strong believer that the retreat is a tool that God uses to reach out to his people. As a team, we are the instruments he uses to connect with the retreatants. We trust in the Holy Spirit, and his guidance is needed to select the appropriate concepts and words to convey his message. I encourage the presenters to give God's talk, not their own. After we have prayed together, I share with the team member the process I use in preparing a talk.

I begin by putting different ideas on 3 x 5 cards. Over the next week or so I jot down things I've found in scripture, magazine articles, a quote, a personal reflection, an inspirational thought, and maybe something that is completely "out of the box." My next step is to review all the ideas I have collected on the 3 x 5's, and select the ones that I feel will be appropriate for this talk. I put the cards in the most logical order, and begin making an outline for the presentation. (I save the cards with ideas I haven't used and they become a nice collection of resource materials for future talks.)

From the outline, I start writing my talk, word for word. Once it is written I read it out loud three or four times, making changes and corrections as I go along, until it feels right. At this time I also time myself. It's surprising to many new team members who have worked and worked on their talk, and discover that it is only three minutes long, or that it goes on for forty-five minutes! After revisions, I practice my final draft two or three times so I can be sure I know the material. Then I begin to reverse the process.

From the final draft I write a new outline, and then transfer the sections of this outline onto 5 x 7 cards that will serve as my notes as I give my talk on the retreat. I find using the note cards keep me focused and on track. I have a great ability to wander from one story to another during a talk without skipping a beat, ending up completely off the topic without making the main point. I use note cards to keep from embarrassing myself and to show mercy for my audience.

I pass this process on to anyone asking for advice on their presentation for two reasons. First to let that person know that, as a youth minister and retreat director who has given dozens of talks at retreats and ministry events, I still labor every time I have to give a presentation. This reinforces the fact that preparing an effective talk takes commitment and a lot of work. Secondly, I go through my process to give them an example of a few steps they can use in writing their talk.

My way is not the only way, but it has worked for me, and if they use my process as a model, it is easier for me to help them along in their preparation process.

After the team has gone through the process of selecting presentation topics, three key steps should be followed in determining the content of the presentation. If time allows, this can be done in broad strokes with the team to better give the presenter a sense of direction the presentation might take. If this isn't possible, it can help the director work with the presenter outside of a retreat team meeting. The three keys I use in helping team members prepare presentations are scope, focus, and target. They are the keys to putting clarity to the content of the talk.

Scope

The first step in determining the content of the presentation is to set limits on the scope of the talk. A presentation on relationships, for example, is too broad. The scope should be limited to one or two types of relationships. Limitations are determined by asking a few key questions:

- ❐ What is the average age of the retreatants?

- ❐ What are the needs of the group?

- ❐ What are the expectations of the group?

- ❐ What is the history of the group?

- ❐ What is the size of the group?

Some of these questions may be hard to answer if you have never worked with this group of retreatants before. If so, the two most important questions you can ask in helping to set the scope for the talk cover the group needs and expectations.

Focus

By setting the focus of the presentation we are choosing the central theme. If we limit the scope of the relation talk, for example, to "Relationships Between Best Friends," our focus then can be on the qualities found in a best friend. The focus must be brief and clear to keep the imaginations of the retreatants from going off in different directions. If we allow the focus to be too broad, the talk can become aimless and boring. Keep the content in focus. Any examples and personal sharing of friendships by the presenter should also stay within the focus of the presentation.

Target

Clarifying the target of the presentation is the most difficult, yet important, aspect of preparing a talk. If the presenter can target the main message of the talk, and then express it in a phrase that is repeated in a few different ways during the retreat presentation, then hopefully all the retreatants get the same message from the talk. The goal is to hit the bull's-eye several times during the presentation to get that target point across.

Reducing the steps in determining the contents of a presentation to scope, focus, and target help to keep clarity in the content. It may sound simplistic, but when a high school junior is preparing a retreat talk for a group of peers, simplicity is the key to lowering the stress level of the presenter and the retreat director.

CRITIQUING TALKS PRIOR TO THE RETREAT

On the retreat, I am not concerned with whether the presenters use notes or even if they have to read part of their talk. I do expect them, when they are giving a personal testimony or telling a story, to look at the audience and tell the story from the heart, not from the page. I also expect them to maintain this eye contact whenever they are emphasizing a main target of the talk.

I want the presenters to be as comfortable as they can be while sharing their story to a room full of peers. I don't care if they stand or sit, and I don't care if they use notes or not. I don't care if they make mistakes, or go too long, or even repeat themselves out of nervousness. I do care that the personal stories they tell are true, and that they believe in what they are saying. I also care that they are able to cover the desired focus of the talk and have a target to emphasize in their talk. This is why we have the team critique the talks before the retreat. During this process I am not afraid to challenge the presenters.

For one retreat, we decided to have a talk on peer pressure, drugs, and alcohol. This talk was to be given by two teens, a boy and a girl, who had four weeks to prepare the talk. As they were presenting the talk before the team for the teams' critique, the eleventh-grade boy revealed in his part of the presentation that he had been drinking with his school friends two or three nights a week since the beginning of summer. He went on to say that he quit drinking the previous weekend, which was to be two weeks before the retreat. During the critique various team members commented that he had covered the subject well, that he was able to stay focused on the central theme, and that he had plenty of personal witness. Then it was my turn to speak.

My concern was whether he truly believed in what he was saying. Did he quit drinking because of the talk and the upcoming retreat, after which he would start drinking again? I asked him if he truly believed he had quit drinking. He said yes. I asked him if his parents knew about his drinking and he said no. I asked him if he had gone to any AA meetings and he said no. I then challenged him to prove to the team and to the retreatants that he believed in what he was saying. "How?" he asked. I told him he had seventy-two hours to talk with his parents about his problem and to go to his first AA meeting. If he could do that, then he would have proven to me and to the team that he was serious about quitting drinking and believed in what he was saying. If he couldn't prove to us that he was serious, then I would be forced to get a new presenter for that talk.

Within forty-eight hours he told his parents about his drinking problem and they took him to his first meeting. He gave his talk on that retreat with genuine conviction. The level of sharing in small groups after that talk was much deeper as a result of the quality of the presentation and the courage of his convictions. (I am happy to say that it has been over ten years since that retreat and that boy, now a man, has remained sober all that time and still attends his meetings. It is with his permission that I share his story.)

I tell this story not to show how tough I can be, but to emphasize how strongly I believe in critiquing talks before the retreat, and that the presenters believe in what they are saying. A room full of teens can pick out a phony after about two minutes. If they question the content or context of a talk, then they begin to question the content of the entire retreat weekend.

I expect retreat talks to be more than just instructional or informative, but to include personal testimony. I believe that personal testimony gives the retreatant the gift of hope. If they see that an adult in the parish or one of their peers had troubles in their lives and are still able to survive and grow in faith from the experience, then it offers hope to the retreatant with their own problems and troubles. Furthermore, hearing others being open and honest about their shortcomings or problems invites the retreatants to be open with their own burdens and receive help and support from peers and youth ministers.

A young adult named Chantal gave one of the best retreat talks I ever heard that offered hope. During the weekend this bright, talented, and gregarious young woman had gained the respect and admiration of all the youth on the retreat. Then, during her talk, she shared her story of losing her father as a teenager and how that changed the path in her life. She told of her struggles with eating disorders, drugs, and alcohol. She ended by saying "That's my story, but I am not my story. I am a person created and loved by God, who has forgiven me for all my sins. He waited patiently for me to turn back to him, and when I did, he welcomed me with open arms. I am not my story. I am a child of God, created to do great things in his name. To love him and my neighbor as I love myself—that's who I am." What a witness of hope she gave those kids that day!

When a person plans to speak about someone else in their personal testimony it is important to get their permission first. Whenever I planned to include a story about one of my children or my wife in a talk I would ask their permission first. When my children were young I would tell them about the talk I was giving for retreats and ask them what they thought I should tell these high school kids. The words of advice from a six, seven, eight or nine-year old child would often serve as the cornerstone of my talks.

If you have a team member who has a family member as a retreatant I advise you to make sure the team member shares the total content of their witness with the retreatant before the retreat. If the retreatant is uncomfortable with any part of the talk it should be removed.

I recently heard the story about a woman who wanted to include a story in her witness about when she was young and made a mistake and had an abortion. She couldn't understand why her freshman son on his first retreat didn't want her to share that part of her story. Always remember that the retreat is for the retreatants, not the team members.

Finally, when the team is finished critiquing the proposed retreat talk, the presenter should have a list of small-group discussion questions ready to be reviewed by the team or director. These are the three or four questions that will be discussed on the retreat in small groups after the presentation, and it is good for the team to be familiar with the questions and to suggest other follow-up topics as well.

Step Eight
CREATING THE CONNECTIONS

☐ Volunteers

☐ Role of the Family

☐ Role of the Parish Community

☐ How to Cultivate Volunteers

VOLUNTEERS

The role of the families, volunteers, and parish community is immeasurable in preparing for a successful retreat experience. The more creative you are and the more aware of the details, the more help you are going to need, and solicit from the community. The art of cultivating a strong list of community volunteers takes a little time and a lot of effort on your behalf, but it's well worth it.

People today have so little time to volunteer and are often so overcommitted that when it comes time to choose a program to devote their time or money to, they most likely will want to associate themselves with a successful program. It is much easier to get support for a proven program than for one that is just starting.

If you don't already have a solid base of support before you start planning your retreat, it could be difficult to get all the help you need. How can you solicit the support you need? I offer some suggestions at the end of this section.

If your goal is to provide a quality, successful retreat experience and not just "do a retreat" because you have to, you are going to need lots of help. Attention to details can leave you worn out before the retreat ever begins. I break my volunteer needs for a retreat into three workable segments; preretreat, retreat, and postretreat volunteers. The volunteers listed here are not necessarily the same people who have volunteered to work on the retreat weekend itself, although the roles sometimes overlap if the volunteer has the time and willingness.

Pre-Retreat Volunteers

☐ Communications

After the retreat applications have been sent out, I have two volunteers help with the follow-up as completed applications begin coming in. Their responsibilities are to send confirmation letters to the parents of the retreatants and final instruction sheets to the retreatants. (Copies of these forms can be found in the appendix.) This team sets up the record keeping to track deposits and final payments. If it gets close to the time of the retreat and a final payment hasn't been received, they call the parents with a friendly reminder. They also make sure I have received an up-to-date medical release form for all retreatants and youth team members.

If they sense any hesitance from the parents about the payment, the volunteer is instructed to inform the parents that scholarship money is available and offer to have me call them. I never want to put a parent or volunteer in an uncomfortable situation, so by offering to have me call the parent makes it easier on everyone. Whenever I call a parent about money, I avoid asking about their situation, and just offer the scholarship up front, telling them that money should never be an issue. I let them know that when it comes to including the youth on retreats I have a list of people willing to help. Of course, I assure them that confidentiality is important and I never tell who the recipient will be when I ask for the money from a donor. I also assure them that I will never mention this to their child or them again. These parents are so grateful for the assistance and some have become my best volunteers. In all my years of youth ministry, only once did I ever feel that a parent took advantage of the situation, but I figured that was between the parent and God. It never stopped me from asking. But my communications team is usually my first line of connection with those families.

❑ *Transportation Coordinator*

This position is only necessary if you are using private vehicles to and from the retreat site. If not, I am a professional and I can order a bus by myself. The purpose of the transportation coordinator is to secure enough drivers and vehicles for all the retreatants, team, and stuff ("stuff" is a ministry term meaning sleeping bags, luggage, food, and supplies) and to make sure that all documentation is complete.

In my diocese, drivers are required to provide proof of insurance and a copy of a valid drivers' license. The coordinator is responsible to collect these documents and to assign passengers to drivers. Finally, this person gives each driver a notebook containing a copy of all the retreatants' medical release forms and permission slips, maps to the retreat center, instructions about times for pick up at the church, and phone numbers of the other drivers' cell phones and of the retreat center. This may seem obvious, but make sure the transportation coordinator also secures transportation for the trip back to the church at the closing of the retreat. Do not automatically assume that a parent who drives a carload to the retreat is also available to pick them up and drive them home. From the voice of experience, always think ahead.

❑ *Banners*

If you are planning to use banners to publicize the retreat or plan to have special banners for the retreat and you are "artistically challenged" like myself, it would be good to get a volunteer for this job. My very talented wife usually provided banners for my retreats and other youth ministry events. The banners usually stayed on the walls in the youth ministry office long after the retreat and were an instant reminder of the retreat experience to all the youth who wandered in and out of the office throughout the weeks to come.

❑ *Shopper*

I rarely use a shopper because I try to anticipate all my needs at the beginning of the year and do one large shopping trip at that time. I buy markers, tape, string, staples, paper, candles, etc. If I need additional items for the retreat, the assistant director does the running around. If you have a large list of supplies you will need for the retreat, get a volunteer who knows where all the best deals are in town and invite him/her to do the shopping for you. I often pick up extra water and snacks for the retreat as well.

❑ *First Aid*

Designate one person on the team as the first-aid person. This person should have a little first-aid training and not be faint at the sight of blood. This person should have the youth ministry first-aid kit handy at all times. If you don't have a youth ministry first-aid kit, get one, keep it well stocked, and bring it with you on all youth ministry events. It should definitely hold more than a few Band-Aids and an ace bandage. Be prepared for anything that could happen away from home. Ask the health care professionals in your parish for advice and donations.

❑ *Contacts*

One person on your team should have a cell phone with him/her at all times for emergencies. This member's number, along with the retreat center phone number, should be given to each retreatant's parents to use in case of emergency. One parent—not on the retreat—should also serve as a communications assistant. This person should have the home phone number of each retreatant. If the bus is delayed in traffic or if there is any kind of problem, this person can be called to get the message out to all the parents. This helps eliminate the problem of worried, frustrated parents sitting in the parking lot of the church waiting two hours for their kids to return from retreat.

Post-Retreat Volunteers

❏ *Closing Mass*

If you have scheduled a special closing Mass or are joining an already scheduled Mass to close the retreat at the parish, get someone to handle the logistics for you. Do you want reserved seating for the retreatants and team? Do you want the retreatants to be a special part of the entrance procession? Will they do the readings? Will they write and lead the prayers of the faithful? Will there be special music? All these things can and should be handled by volunteers who are not on the retreat itself.

❏ *Potluck*

If your retreat ends in the parish hall with a family potluck dinner after which the retreatants can share their retreat experiences, get a team to plan the dinner, make the calls, set up the hall, and, most importantly, do the cleanup.

ROLE OF THE FAMILY

The parents and family are the primary educators of faith for their children. My role as youth minister is to support what should be taking place in the home. With this in mind, I request that parents support what I am doing by encouraging their children to take full advantage of the opportunity available to them on retreat.

At times I have asked parents to be more supportive and forgiving of their child in the days leading up to a retreat. This helps the youth on the weekend, knowing that their parents are behind them. It also makes it a little easier when a child comes home after a good retreat experience, knowing he is coming home to a loving and peaceful environment.

Occasionally, I request the parents and family to write a supportive, loving letter for their child on retreat. This letter is given to the retreatants as a surprise at the end of a spiritual exercise. I feel so strongly about these letters that the parents are required to have these letters in my office three days before the retreat. It's not unusual to have a high-school senior boy so profoundly touched by his parent letter that he tells me in tears it's the first time his dad has ever told him he loved him.

Parents are also required to attend any closing liturgy or celebration at the church after the retreat. The parents go to the kids' soccer games or dance recitals. This is more important and strongly supports the faith decisions the youth have made on retreat. I ask that siblings attend as well. When younger children see high-school kids excited about their faith and openly expressing their love for God, it sets the stage of anticipation for when they get to high school and get to go on a retreat. It also sends the message that being a Christian is a "cool" thing that they can be proud of.

I encourage parents to be sensitive to the mood of the retreatants after they get home following a retreat. Most parents are anxious to ask a shopping list of questions about the retreat when their child gets home. My experience has been that most kids need a day or two to process the experience before they can verbalize it.

As you can tell, I expect a lot from the families before, during, and after a retreat. My goal through all these expectations is that it will open the channels of communication between the parents and their kids. With these communication channels open, my expectations are that the parents will have an opportunity to talk about their own faith journey with their children.

ROLE OF THE PARISH COMMUNITY

For weeks before the retreat, I place announcements in the bulletin asking the parish to pray for the success of the upcoming retreat. Before we leave for the retreat I submit a prayer to be added to the prayers of the faithful at Mass, which brings the entire parish community to pray for the retreat during the weekend. I also invite the entire parish to join us for our closing Mass after the retreat. I let them know that the Mass might be a little longer than usual, but for those who choose to come, it blesses them to see the youth on fire in their faith.

HOW TO CULTIVATE VOLUNTEERS

If you are in the building phase of a successful youth ministry program, you may find it hard for people to be willing to give you part of their limited free time or assets. If you find this to be true, and they are not willing to give your program their time, then you have to change your approach and their thinking. By this I mean not to ask them to help with the program but to help you achieve the building of the program.

You might find out that there are many parishioners who believe in what you want to do, but feel uncomfortable working with teenagers, or just never considered it before. If you can convey a sense of confidence in your vision and are able to lay out very clearly your plans to achieve this vision, the only thing remaining is to be able to explain to them exactly and specifically how they can help you, either directly with the youth, or from the sidelines. The only thing left to do is to ask. Many people just forget to ask. "Do you think you can help me achieve my vision of youth ministry for our parish?"

If you are confident and have a clear vision for your program and are specific in how others can help you, then "no" is a tough response to give. If they do say that they are very much in support of you and your vision but are unable to help you at this time, ask them when a better time might be. Six months? Eight months? Next year? When? If they are unable to make any commitment about time but still want to help, ask if you can call on them in the future to help financially with the program or to provide scholarship money for a youth group member to go on retreat or to another youth ministry event.

Once you are confident that your vision is marketable and you are not afraid to ask for help, start making two lists. One list is for those who are willing to help with their time and one for those who are willing to help with their treasure. As the success of your program grows, your lists will grow as well. Eventually you will not have to ask any more, just take names of volunteers. If your vision is successful, people will begin coming to you and asking how they can help.

Once you have volunteers, don't lose them by taking them for granted. Send thank-you cards, take them to dinner or lunch, send flowers when appropriate, show them they are appreciated. When I was in full-time ministry, my wife and I would host two parties a year for my volunteers; one around Christmas time, and the other at the end of the school year. It was a great opportunity to show our gratitude for the gifts of time, talent, and treasure they shared with the youth throughout the year.

Once a volunteer has said yes, the next step is yours. At one parish I received an envelope with a check in it for $100 with a note that said "for the youth group." I called the lady who sent it and thanked her personally for the donation. During the course of our conversation she offered to help again in the future. She said all I had to do was call . . . and I did. Her generosity helped with scholarship funds for quite a few kids to many youth ministry functions. One event I called her about was World Youth Day in Denver in 1993. I had about sixty-five people going and ten of the kids needed help with the $400 cost of the trip. I called and explained to her about World Youth Day, the cost of the event, and the ten kids who needed financial help, and asked if she would be able to help a kid or two. She was very excited about World Youth Day and the opportunity for the kids to see the pope. She told me that she would be in my office with her checkbook within a week. She was in my office the next morning with her check for $4,000, covering the cost for all ten kids. I thanked her and told her that some of the kids had already raised some of their money and didn't need the full amount. She informed me that she met the pope in 1986 and was born in Denver, and that she wanted to cover the entire cost for those ten kids, and any money they had already raised could be used for spending money in Denver.

Upon our return, each of these grateful kids wrote a personal thank-you letter to their benefactor. Anne passed away a few years ago, and because of her generosity to the youth group of our parish, I'm certain God was waiting at the gates of heaven to thank her in person as well.

Conclusion
CREATING THE EXPERIENCE

◻ Putting It All Together

PUTTING IT ALL TOGETHER

Early in my career as a youth minister, when I first began putting together the framework for *Creating a Successful Youth Retreat*, I drew on many resources for help. My experience in Cursillo and Marriage Encounter and personal retreats all were very helpful. Having friends who I could call on for advice and support like Kevin Buck and Joyce Cottage, both of whom are excellent role models and retreat directors, was invaluable. Drawing from all those resources, I still made mistakes along the way. But I didn't quit trying to improve on the retreats I directed. I learned from my mistakes and improved the process until the formula worked well in all retreat situations.

I strongly believe that the greatest gift we can give to the youth in our programs, or to anyone desiring a closer relationship with God is a retreat experience that is well planned and executed. A good retreat should be well balanced between large-group and small-group time. The talks, prayer experiences, spiritual exercises, and activities should flow into and out of each other with ease and purpose. The talks should build on each other and be easily connected to accent the theme. The games, icebreakers, and community builders should be used sparingly and with purpose.

Getting the details of the final retreat schedule worked out can be a challenge. As I work toward a final schedule, I ask myself these questions: Is it covering the needs of the group? Is it balanced? Is it building toward a purpose? Are the presentations in the proper order? Do I have enough time allocated for sharing? Are there enough breaks and free time? Are most of the concerns of the team covered? Once I have complete satisfaction that the schedule is ready to go, I present it to the team for final approval. Keep in mind that as the director you have the final word over the schedule. If a suggestion is made by a team member to change the schedule, take their suggestion and pray about it. If, after much thought and prayer you feel good about making the change, then do so. If you don't, then thank the team member for their idea and explain why you didn't make the change. Remember, as the retreat director you are ultimately responsible for the success of the retreat.

Now would be a good time to emphasize again the power of prayer in planning and executing a powerful retreat experience. As I wrote earlier in the book, a retreat is one way for God to touch the lives of his people in a very meaningful way. The director and team are God's tools during the retreat. With this basic belief I go to the Holy Spirit for guidance and direction before I make any major decisions concerning the planning phase of any retreat experience.

I pray before I select the team. I pray for guidance in choosing a theme and topics for talks. I pray that the Holy Spirit will guide me to the right people to give a talk or presentation. I pray that the prayer services, spiritual exercises, and liturgy are fulfilling in the spiritual lives of the retreatants. I pray that the games, icebreakers, and community builders do the job they were intended to do. I pray that God is already preparing the hearts of the retreatants to hear his word and receive his love. Finally, I pray that the Holy Spirit shower the whole team with all the gifts and fruits of the Spirit needed to do God's work. It is prayer and guidance from the Holy Spirit that makes a retreat successful. The director has to be open to the winds of the Spirit, and then be ready to work.

For one weekend retreat I kept a log of how much time I put into the preparation before the actual retreat. My final tally was just over two hundred hours. Now some may agree that this is a lot of time spent on one element of youth ministry, especially if you do two or three retreats a year. I have to agree. This is a lot of time, but for me no other element in my ministry is as effective in bringing kids to a profound experience of a better relationship with God than a retreat. Where else in ministry do you get the opportunities to make a lasting impression with so many souls in a concentrated time frame than on a retreat?

The more time I spend in training the team and fine-tuning the framework for the retreat, the better experience the retreatants have. Planning and covering the details and asking the tough questions before the retreat assure a smoother running retreat for you as the director.

In conclusion, I would encourage you to do a follow-up night shortly after the retreat. This gives the retreatants and the team the opportunity to come together one last time to share about the retreat and what life is like for them now that they are back. I always do this at the first regularly scheduled youth group meeting after the retreat (which for me is Tuesday nights). This works out to be a great night for three reasons. First, it is already on the youths' calendars as a youth ministry night and they are already tuned in to come to the church. Second, it gives those who were unable to attend the retreat a chance to get a flavor of the retreat experience and plant the seed that they shouldn't miss the next one. Third, it gives me, as the youth minister/retreat director, a full night of activities and sharing without much work just coming off of the retreat. Some might see this as a little selfish; others might see it as the voice of experience. Whatever the reason, enjoy the glow only a retreat can produce for as long as you can. Working with youth, you know that tomorrow brings a whole new set of challenges.

Appendix
FORMS AND
OTHER RESOURCES

- ☐ Creating Your Resources

- ☐ Retreat Schedule

- ☐ Retreat Application

- ☐ Retreat Application Form

- ☐ General Retreat Information Form

- ☐ Sample Letter to Parents

- ☐ Sample Letter to Retreatants

- ☐ Checklist for Directors

- ☐ More Resources

CREATING YOUR RESOURCES

One of my most valuable tools is the resource file I have developed over the years. Just as my family has kept photo albums and souvenirs of places we have visited, as I have journeyed in my ministry, I have kept copies of talks I have written, notes from presentations I have attended, interesting articles, hand-outs, stories, etc. Although I can honestly say that in my twenty-plus years of ministry I have never given the exact talk twice, I am often asked to speak to groups, and some topics such as "The Gifts of the Spirit" are frequent requests. I always put a new spin on the talk, or approach it from a different angle, but my resource file is the first place I look for inspiration and ideas.

Also in my resource file are copies of all the forms, journals, and letters I have used for retreats. As with my presentations, I try to customize the forms for each retreat, incorporating the theme of the weekend into the letter and clip-art. This is particularly important to retreatants who have been on retreat before. They can immediately see by the look of the form that this retreat will be different from their last retreat, and they will be more likely to sign up.

I have included some general forms and letters that I have used. My goal is not that you would copy them and use them word-for-word, but that they will serve as useful frameworks as you design the paperwork for your retreats. I also hope that these will be useful additions to your new or already existing file of resources.

RETREAT SCHEDULE

FRIDAY:

3:30   Team arrives at church
(Advance team already at retreat center)
Set up at church for arrival of retreatants

Greeters: _____

_____

Logistics: _____

_____

Luggage: _____

_____

_____

_____

Bus Captain:_____

_____

4:00   Retreatants arrive at church

4:30   Bus leaves for retreat center
   ❒ Eat dinner on bus

7:30   Arrive at retreat center
   ❒ Unload busses and set up in dorms
   ❒ Snacks and drinks

8:00   Introduction and Orientation—given by Director
      ❐ Welcome
      ❐ What is a retreat?
      ❐ Expectations, cooperation, and confidentiality
      ❐ Rules and regulations (Mark's two rules)
      ❐ Introduce team
      ❐ Theme and theme song: _____

      ❐ Opening Prayer: _____

8:30   Name tags and large-group icebreakers

      _____

      _____

9:15   Break into small groups / Small-group community builders

      _____

      _____

10:00   Break

10:10   First talk: _____
      By: _____
          (Team prays over speaker)

      ❐ Silent reflection

10:30   Small group sharing

10:50   Night Prayer _____

11:05   Bedtime

11:25   Lights Out

SATURDAY

7:00   Wake-up call

8:00   Breakfast

8:45   Team meeting

9:00   Morning Prayer _____

9:15   Large group games

        _____

        _____

9:45   Prayer Partners

        _____

        _____

10:00   Small group games / Community builders

10:15   Break

10:30   Second talk: _____

        By: _____

            (Team prays over speaker)

10:50   Reflection

10:55   Small-group sharing

11:45   Break

12:00   Lunch, free time

2:30   Gathering _____

        _____

2:45   Third talk: _____

        By: _____
            (Team prays over speaker)

3:05   Reflection

3:10   Small group sharing / Set up for Mass

4:05   Break

4:15   Spiritual Exercise: _____

        By: _____
            (Spiritual groups)

5:10   Mass   _____

                 _____

6:15   Dinner   _____*Décor for special dinner?*_____

                 _____*Costumes?*_____

7:30   Skits   _____

                 _____

9:25   Break

9:30   Fourth talk: _____

        By: _____
        (Team prays over speaker)

9:55   Reflection

10:00   Sharing

11:00   Parent Letters

11:30   Bedtime

11:45   Lights out

SUNDAY:

7:30   Wake-up call

8:30   Breakfast, pack belongings

9:30   Morning Prayer _____

9:45   Fifth talk: _____

        By: _____
            (Team prays over speaker)

10:10   Affirmation circles

12:15   Lunch and clean-up

1:30   Sixth talk: _____

        By: _____
            (Team prays over speaker)

2:00   Summary, prayer partners, and prayer service

        _____

        _____

3:00   Board busses

6:00   Closing Mass at church
        (Often followed by a potluck at the church hall)

RETREAT APPLICATION

Get Ready!

Our next retreat will be _____ , and

YOU ARE INVITED!

All youth in the program are invited, but those preparing for Confirmation are required to attend two retreats, and this retreat will fulfill one of these.

This retreat will be limited to _____ participants. Space is reserved on a "first come, first served" basis, so be sure to return your application as soon as possible. There will be a waiting list.

The total cost (food, transportation, lodging, etc.) for the weekend is only $_____. Your application and non refundable deposit are due by _____. Please return the attached application to the youth ministry office only.

Financial assistance is available. Please call me at _____.

(See next page)

RETREAT APPLICATION FORM

Youth Ministry Retreat:

_____
When   Where

Name _____

Address _____

City / State / Zip _____

Mother's Name _____ Daytime Phone_____

Father's Name _____ Daytime Phone_____

How would you describe your relationship with God? _____
_____

If you were made pope, what would be the first thing you would
change in the church?_____
_____

Have you been on a retreat before? When? _____
_____

What do you think are the biggest social problems facing youth today?
_____

What topics would you personally like covered this weekend? _____
_____

What are your interests? (clubs, sports, school, music, dance, . . .)
_____

    Parent's signature: _____

GENERAL RETREAT INFORMATION FORM

Name: _____

            Last   First   Middle

Address: _____

            Street   City   Zip

School: _____ Grade: _____

Age: _____ Birthday: _____/_____/_____

Parents' Names: _____

                        Father

               _____

                        Mother

Deposit: _____ Balance: _____

Letter: _____/_____

                To   From

Medical Release Form: _____

_____

Small Group: _____

SAMPLE LETTER TO PARENTS

Date ____/____/_____

Dear Parents:

The team for the upcoming Youth Ministry Retreat has been working for months to create a very special retreat experience for your child. The theme for the weekend is _____ _____, and we have planned a full schedule of activities for the retreatants. The retreat will be at ____*retreat center name*____ (*phone number*) and you will play an important part of what happens before, during, and after the retreat.

Before the retreat, you can help by encouraging your child to go on this retreat with an open heart and mind, and reminding them that they are going not just to be with their friends, but also to experience God.

During the retreat we will have a talk and reflection on the importance of family. After this talk we have set aside time that in the past has been considered a highlight for virtually all of the youth. This is the moment when we give the retreatants love letters from their parents and family. This is where we need your help. Please write a personal letter to your child that is a positive expression of your love, and an affirmation of your child's important role in your family. The letters can be any length you like, and they will be confidential, to be read only by your child. Letters from siblings, grandparents, etc., are encouraged as well.

The letter(s) are a *surprise*, so please don't tell your child about it or give the letters to your child to bring to the retreat. You must bring the letters in person to the youth ministry office or parish rectory by _____*date*_____. If you leave it at the parish rectory, please clearly write "High School Retreat" on the envelope. We regard this moment on the retreat as so important that your child will not be able to go on the retreat if you have not turned in your letter(s).

After the retreat, on _____*date*_____, we will return to the church for our concluding celebration of the weekend. We ask that you and your family join us in this celebration at the _____*time*_____ Mass. Your participation will make it even more special for your child. Plan to be at the church early to welcome our retreatants home.

Please pray for us during our retreat. Thank you in advance for your help and participation. If you have any questions, please call me at ___*phone*___.

In his service,

_____
Signature

CONFIDENTIAL!
DO NOT SHARE THIS INFORMATION
WITH YOUR CHILD!

SAMPLE LETTER TO RETREATANTS

Date ____/____/_____

Dear Retreatant,

On behalf of the retreat team, welcome to our newest retreat, ____*retreat name*____. Your retreat team has been meeting for two months in preparation for your retreat experience, and we will rely on your cooperation and loving spirit to accomplish all that we have planned for you. We have been praying for each of you. Please pray for us as well.

The first thing to remember is that this weekend is for you and God; not for you and your friends. Try to focus your thoughts on your relationship with God this weekend. I hope that you are all praying with us and asking God to make this a memorable weekend for all of us. It will only be a success for you if you come to the weekend with an open mind and open heart.

Here's your checklist of what to bring:

- ❏ Warm sleeping bag and pillow
- ❏ Enough clothes for a weekend
- ❏ Heavy jacket or coat
- ❏ Change of shoes for hiking
- ❏ Flashlight
- ❏ Towel, washcloth, soap, and toiletries
- ❏ Warm socks

❒ Dinner to eat on the bus

❒ Snack food to share on the weekend (no food will be allowed in the dorms)

Here's your checklist of what to leave at home:

❒ Watches

❒ Radio, Walkman, laptops, cell phones, palm pilots, pagers, etc.

❒ Homework

❒ Bad attitudes

❒ CD's and Tapes

(If you bring any of these, they will be taken from you for the weekend.)

Please, Please, Please be at the church on ___*day*___, ___*date*___, at ___*time*___. We cannot hold up the bus and the entire group if you are late.

The team is waiting to serve you. God bless you and have a great weekend!

In his service,

_____
Signature

CHECKLIST FOR DIRECTORS

Things to Bring:

- ☐ Pens
- ☐ Pencils
- ☐ Tape
- ☐ Scissors
- ☐ Colored paper
- ☐ Lined paper
- ☐ Markers and crayons
- ☐ Magazines for cut-and-paste
- ☐ Candles
- ☐ Matches
- ☐ Flowers for environment
- ☐ Supplies for environment
- ☐ Extra cups
- ☐ Kleenex (at least one box per group)
- ☐ Bibles
- ☐ Props for skits
- ☐ Decorations for dining room
- ☐ Camera
- ☐ Film
- ☐ Video camera and tripod
- ☐ Name tags
- ☐ Words to songs

- ☐ Sound system (if needed)
- ☐ CD/Tape player for outdoor services
- ☐ Tapes and CD's
- ☐ Maps to and from retreat center
- ☐ Questions for talks 1 through 7
- ☐ List of rules and regulations
- ☐ Prayer partner information
- ☐ Supplies for Mass
- ☐ Supplies for prayer services
- ☐ List of retreatants
- ☐ Parent letters
- ☐ Medical release forms for each vehicle
- ☐ Snacks
- ☐ Critique forms
- ☐ Bell or whistle to gather retreatants
- ☐ Thank-you cards for team

And Just in Case:

- ☐ Extra pillows, and blankets
- ☐ Extra toothbrushes
- ☐ Extra toiletries, including feminine products
- ☐ First-aid kit
- ☐ Extra games and community builders
- ☐ Extra prayer services
- ☐ Backup sound system

MORE RESOURCES

I have used many resources through the years, but there are a few that come to mind that I have been able to draw from over and over again:

Art of Christian Listening, The. Hart, Thomas N. Paulist Press, Mahwah, New Jersey, 1981.

Best of Play It, The. Rice, Wayne and Yaconelli, Mike, editors, (Youth Specialties) Zondervan, Grand Rapids, Michigan, 2000.

Book of Uncommon Prayer, The. Case, Steve, Youth Specialties, Zondervan, Grand Rapids, Michigan, 2002.

Earth Prayers from Around the World. Amidon, Elias L. and Roberts, Elizabeth. J. Harper SanFrancisco, 1991.

Gigantic Book of Games for Youth Ministry, The, volumes 1 and 2. McLaughlin, Dennis R. and Anthony, Michelle, editors. Group Publishing, Loveland, Colorado, 1999.

Groupbuilder Games and Activities for Youth Ministry. Group Publishing, Loveland, Colorado, 2000.

Crowd Breakers & Mixers: The Ideas Library. Youth Specialties. Zondervan, Grand Rapids, Michigan, 1997.

Ideas: Games, Games II and Games III. Youth Specialties. Zondervan, Grand Rapids, Michigan, 2002.

Out of the Ordinary: Prayers, Poems, and Reflections for Every Season. Rupp, Joyce. Ave Maria Press, Notre Dame, Indiana, 2000.